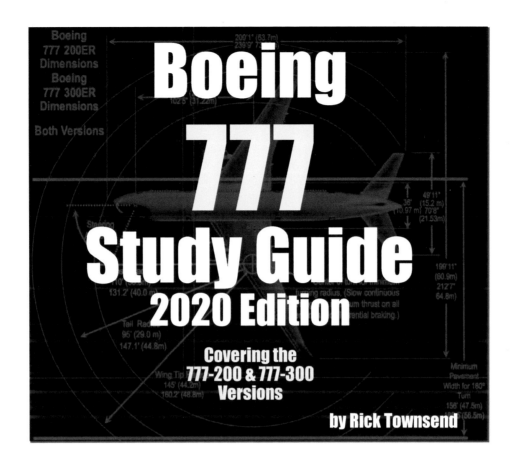

This book was originally developed for pilots at American Airlines. Neither American Airlines nor Boeing Corporation have endorsed or in any way been responsible for the content of this book.

As a courtesy to the pilots of American Airlines who have supported the development of these books, it is noted that this edition is current to the best ability of the author to make it so, and includes material relevant to:

QRH Revision 38, Temporary Revision— None
Operating Manual Volume I Revision 91.2, Temporary Revision — None
Operating Manual Volume II Revision 12, Temporary Revision — None
Performance Manual Revision 25, Temporary Revision — None

Abbreviations used in this book:
Operating Manual Volume I — OMV1
Operating Manual Volume II — OMV2
Performance Manual — PERF
Quick Review Handbook — QRH

Revision Notes

September 18, 2019 Edition

Revision notes are summarized from the initial issue of this book in January 2019 through the current edition.

> Page i: Content updated to reflect changes to manufacturers' or airlines' newly revised operating manual updates. Specifically,
> Boeing 777 Quick Reference Handbook was updated from Revision 35 to revision 37.
> Boeing 777 Operating Manual Vol. I was updated from Revision 88 to revision 90
> Boeing 777 OMV2 was updated from Revision 10 to revision 11
> Performance Manual was updated from Revision 22 to revision 23.

> Page 1: Graphic inserted and Table of Contents Reflowed for readability

November 5, 2019 Edition
> Page 8—Added broadband COMM switch requirement to be off during deicing operations on the ground.
> Removed WLAN cockpit restriction from -200 series aircraft
> Page 9—APU Starter limitations revised
> Page 14—Reworded "Captain" column, "after 60 knots" section to include new thrust lever nomenclature.
> Criteria for rejected takeoff expanded to include predictive windshear caution

November 24, 2019 Edition
> Page 4—Added Broadband switch to overhead panel diagram
> Page 19—Added takeoff flap selection information

December 26, 2019 Edition
> Page 6—New Wind Limitations chart incorporates data from multiple places in the other operating guidance manuals.
> Newly copyrighted edition for 2020

March 19, 2020 Edition
> Page 19 & Page 61—Tailwind wording removed from Standard Thrust on Takeoff requirements list
> Page 19—AC to Pack Takeoff section added
> Several references to FM Part I updated to FOM reference paragraphs.

Published by Pilot Study Guides, LLC, Grapevine, Texas.
First Edition and Copyright 2004
Updated continuously (including copyright protection) through the current 2019 edition.

Graphics: With one exception, all graphics were produced by and are the copyright-protected property of the author, except where noted within this edition.

Acknowledgement: Thanks to Norebbo Design Studios, *www.norebbo.com* for allowing use of the profile drawing in the *Airplane General* section.

Corporation References: American Airlines™ and the Boeing Corporation™, referenced herein, have neither endorsed nor provided any proprietary information for use in these books. Their referencing is for informational awareness only.

ISBN: **978-1-946544-27-8** (Print)
ISBN: **978-1-946544-32-2** (Amazon Kindle)

Table of Contents

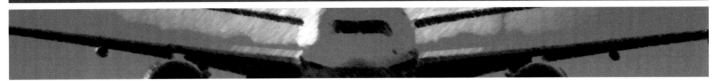

Introduction

What This Book IS

This Study Guide is a compilation of notes taken primarily from the flight manual, but also includes elements taken from class notes, computer-based training, and operational experience. It is intended for use by initial qualification crewmembers preparing for orals, and also for systems review prior to recurrent training or check rides. It is assembled in an attempt to organize in one location all the buzz words, acronyms, and numbers the average guy needs to know in order to get through the events above from an aircraft systems standpoint.

What this Book IS NOT

This series of books was originally developed for use by American Airlines pilots. It is for that purpose that operating manual references are for the manual sets for that airline as a courtesy to my loyal customers of many years. The books **are _not_** officially sanctioned in any way by any airline, however. The author assumes all responsibility for accuracy. (Forward corrections to the address provided, please!)

These books **do not** replace study of the operations manual, but instead provide a supplementary source of review material to complement study of official publications. Except for a few specific areas, it does not include regulatory guidance or other materials—just airplane systems details, some ideas for organizing the cockpit flow, cold weather operations, etc. The Study Guide is not printed on fancy paper or expensively bound. That makes it easy to tuck into your kit bag or briefcase and study as you travel. Therefore, for these same reasons, it is far less expensive than most commercially produced books of its kind. It is intended to be affordable and usable.

Suggested Uses

A good time to use this book is on layovers. A reasonable plan would be to attempt to review limitations, memorization Red Box items once per sequence, and the rest of the sections once per month. Reviewing sectional study outlines usually leads to trying to remember one of those great plumbing diagrams from the flight manual or synoptics, and so those also get reviewed in the process.

Limitations and Black Border items are laid out so that you may cover the answer with a 3x5 card and quiz yourself. Other sections are in outline form.

A word about acronyms—you will probably see most of the acronyms you have heard of before in this booklet, as well as a few new ones. Most of us avoid them when possible, using clues on aircraft instrument and systems management panels to jog our memories. But for those you have trouble with, I've included all the ones I could think of. It is not necessary to learn all of them, but only those you need to help remember tough sets of items. Thankfully, the 777 fleet management folks believe in keeping these "laundry lists" to a minimum, so you will see fewer of these than you will likely have seen in previous aircraft types.

Unique Formatting Features

Throughout this book, several specific methods are used to highlight information. They include:

Recommended memorization sections

A key feature in the study guide includes highlighting information which is recommended for memorization. These are areas that have been asked on orals or which simply need to be known without reference to the books. This new feature is found in systems notes, but not in the limitations section, which all requires a high level of retention. If you have recommendations for information that should be so highlighted but is not, please let me know and I will do so in a future version.

Master Caution and Master Warning lights are Indicated by highlighted **MC** (Master Caution) and **MW** (Master Warning) highlights within this Guide.

Panel or Warning Light Text—Words or indications found on system panels or switches is indicated by bold, all capital letters such as **LOW PRESSURE**.

300ER Series data has been included throughout this book. Editorial decisions have been made about how much **300ER** data to include. Your inputs are gratefully accepted.

Aircraft versions are indicated in this guide where differences occur with the notation **200ER** or **300ER**. Where not specified, data pertains to both aircraft models. Only where it is different will the identifying tags be used. Thanks for your assistance in letting me know if you feel additional data on **300ER** models should be included or corrected.

Electronic Version

An electronic version of this study material is also available. Buttons at the top of each page represent functions available in the iBooks version of this study guide (iPad/smart phone) to return to the Table of Contents or panel drawings. See web site for details.

| Table of Contents | Overhead Panel | Fwd Panel Ctr Console |

The corner boxes on each page identify the book section and are not hyperlinked.

Panel drawing pages show graphics which are described in this book. Clicking on or touching the colored graphic panels in electronic versions of this book moves to the page with that graphic and its description.

Green shaded areas are not depicted or discussed in this book.

Reproduction

Please don't photocopy this book. I have made a serious effort to keep the costs low for you. In fact, you can buy this book for about half the price of comparable material offered through other commercial publishers. There is a lot of work in this book, as you'll soon be able to see when you study the material. Pages with notes, when provided and annotated as such, may be freely copied by customers. Thanks for your cooperation.

Again, please send me any suggestions or corrections using the contact information below:

Rick Townsend ....Grapevine, Texas
....(817) 416-5533
E-Mail... _rick@pilotstudyguide.com_
Web Site...................................... _www.PilotStudyGuide.com_

Revisions & Subscriptions

Revisions are made on a regular basis. The downside of revisions is that updating your digital version causes you to lose highlighting and notes you have made. This is because each version includes a change to the printing date, so each page is updated on every new release. The methods for updating digital versions varies by platform. See the Pilot Study Guide web site for details.

To contact the Flight Academy Gift Shop and have a book mailed to your home, you may use the following:

Office 817-967-5540
Via Internet................................. _www.crewoutfitters.com_

Publication Details

Compiled: August 3, 2020

For ISBN and additional publication details, see title page

Panels

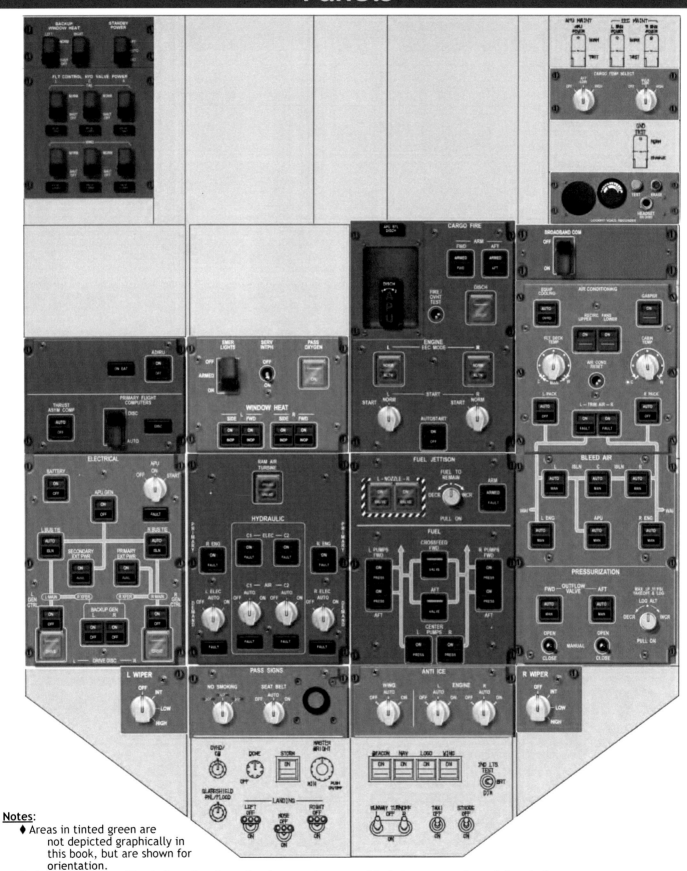

Notes:
- ♦ Areas in tinted green are not depicted graphically in this book, but are shown for orientation.
- ♦ Electronic version: Touch the colored panel to jump to the page with that system and panel description.

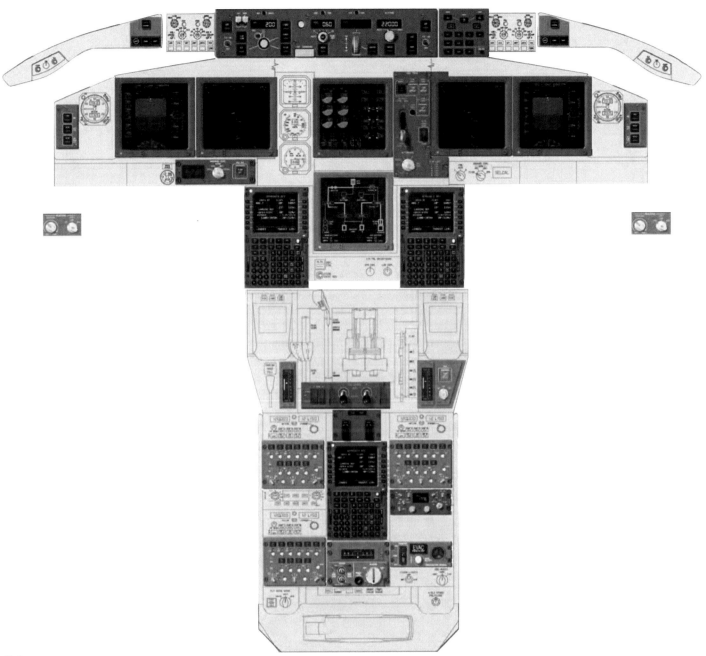

Notes:
♦ Areas in tinted green are not depicted graphically in this book, but are shown for orientation.
♦ Electronic version: Touch the colored panel to jump to the page with that system and panel description.

Limitations

This Section is laid out for study with system areas on one side and the appropriate limitation on the other, so you can cover the answer with an index card and quiz yourself. Some of the limitations in Section 2 are not often encountered, such as alternate fuel limitations. For that reason, they have been shortened here for study. These will be listed in the left column, so that as you study, you will be reminded the limitation exists in the book and will (hopefully) think to look there should the situation be encountered. The Limitation column contains only a reminder to check the Ops Manual for the item in question.

Memorization items are outlined with a dashed line similar to the outline used in the operating manual.

Crewmembers are required to be familiar with all items covered by a limitation. fleet does not have memorization dashed boxes in the Limitations section, however.

Items formatted with green background are limiting guidance from other sections of the operating manual or Flight Operations Manual (FOM). They are included in this section for ease of study.

All items pertain to all models unless indicated to be different with the model tags **200ER** and **300ER**.

General Limitations (AFM)

Applicable to Aircraft Type:	777-200ER and 777-300ER airplanes
Required Flight Crew:	Pilot, Copilot
Airplane Configuration:	Configurations specified in OM for flight regimes are those on which performance section data are based. Prescribed configurations must be used to assure the airplane performance requirements will be met.
Types of airplane Operation:	Airplane approved by the FAA for both day and night in visual, instrument, icing, and extended over water operations.
Certification Status:	The 777 is certified in Transport Category, FAR Part 25 & FAR Part 36.

Operational Limitations (AFM)

Center of Gravity Limits:		Compliance with center of gravity (CG) limits is assured by operations under an approved Weight Control System.
Tires (AFM)	Compliance with Size, minimum load and ply rating:	Assured by operation under the General Procedures Manual (GPM) and Illustrated Parts Catalog (IPC)
Brakes (AFM)	Compliance with part numbers:	Assured by operation under the Illustrated Parts Catalog (IPC)
	Brake Inspection Required:	Following any abort in which maximum (RTO) braking was used or any high speed rejected takeoff (>80 Knots) QRH Maneuvers 1.12

Flight Maneuvering Load Acceleration Limits (AFM)

Flaps Up:	+2.5 to -1.0G	**Note**: With flaps 25 and 30, positive limits vary
Flaps Down:	+2.0 to 0.0 G	linearly from +2.0g at maximum landing weight to +1.5 g at maximum takeoff weight.

Wind Limitations (Knots)	B777-200ER	B777-200ER	Notes
Tailwind Component	10	15	May be reduced by performance requirements
Demonstrated Crosswind		38	All wind limits include gusts.
Autoland—Headwind		25	
Autoland—Tailwind	10	15	Crosswind components at these values with higher gusts should be considered operationally unacceptable.
Autoland—Crosswind		15	
Takeoff Crosswind Limits			
Dry		38	The captain may choose to further reduce this limit based on such factors as gust velocity, runway width/length, braking action and weather.
Wet		38	
Standing Water/Slush		25	
Snow (Wet & Dry)		25	
Compacted Snow		65	**300ER** For ground operation (exclusive of takeoff) in tailwinds and crosswinds between 30 and 45 knots, engine power should be limited to a maximum of 70% N1. Avoid thrust levels above that required for normal taxi operations in all tailwinds and crosswinds greater than 45 knots.
Ice		15	
Landing Crosswind Limits			
6—Dry		38	
5—Good		38	
4—Good to Medium		35	
3—Medium		25	
2—Medium to Poor		17	Wind limits may be further restricted by Non-Normal procedures, crew restrictions (FOM), or less than normal runway width as specified on Ops Advisory pages (##-7).
1—Poor		15	
Miscellaneous			
All Doors—Opening or Closing		40	
All Doors—While Open		65	
Visibility Less than 3/4 SM (RVR 4000) (1200 Meters)—Max Crosswind—Landing		15	Reduce crosswind limits by 5 knots on wet or contaminated runways whenever asymmetric reverse thrust is used.
Peak Wind Value - Except in an Emergency		50	

Runway less than standard width (148 feet / 45 meters):	20 knots	FOM 5g.1.4
Runway Limit (AFM) Runway Slope:	±2%	

T/O, Landing & Enroute Altitude Limits (AFM)

Maximum Certification Altitude, Flight:	43,100 Feet
Max Certification Altitude, T/O & Landing:	8,400 Feet

Autobrake Requirements

When Required:
- Runway <7000'
- RVR <4000' or visibility <3/4 mile (1200m)
- Runway contaminated with standing water, snow, slush, or ice
- Braking conditions less than good
- Approach speed increased above normal by procedure.

When Recommended: Landing with gusty winds or crosswinds.   OMV1, APP-LDG-G/A-15.2

Airspeed (AFM)

Maximum Airspeed Limits

	200ER	**300ER**
V_{MO}:	330 Knots IAS	330-350 Knots IAS
		(Varies by altitude, see chart below)
M_{MO}:	0.87 Mach	0.89 Mach
Determined By:	Lower edge of red and black colored region of the speed tape on the Primary Flight Displays (PFD).	

Limits shall not be deliberately exceeded in any regime of flight

Landing Gear

| Operating (V_{LO} / M_{LO}): | 270 Kts.82 M |
| Extended (V_{LE} / M_{LE}): | 270 Kts.82 M |

Flaps

Maximum Pressure Altitude for Operating with Flaps Extended: 20,000 Feet

Placard Speeds—(AFM)

Position	V_{FE} (Knots)	
	200ER	**300ER**
1:	255	265
5:	235	245
15:	215	230
20:	195	225
25:	185	200
30:	170	180

200ER

300ER

V_A Definition: Speed above which maneuvers should be avoided which involve:
- Full application of rudder, ailerons or elevator, *OR*
- Angles of attack near stall

Turbulence Penetration Speed

For Severe Turbulence	<25,000':	270 KIAS
	≥25,000'—The Lower of:	• 280 KIAS *OR*
		• Mach 0.82

But in all cases: ≥ *25,000':* Maintain a minimum speed of 15 knots above the minimum maneuvering speed (amber band) at all altitudes when the airspeed is below 0.82 Mach.

Weight (AFM)

	300ER	**200ER**
Maximum Taxi Weight (AFM):	777,000 lbs.	650,000 lbs.
Maximum Takeoff Weight (AFM):	775,000 lbs.	648,000 lbs.
Maximum Landing Weight (AFM):	554,000 lbs.	460,000 lbs.
Maximum Zero Fuel Weight (AFM):	524,000 lbs.	430,000 lbs.
Minimum In-flight Weight (AFM):	305,500 lbs.*	266,100 lbs.* *Does not include usable fuel

Notes: Landing at any weight that exceeds the Maximum Landing Weight is defined as an overweight landing. Refer to FOM 11n.2 for the overweight landing policy, QRH Miscellaneous 0.31 for the Overweight Landing Checklist, and to FOM 1M.11 for AML Writeup requirements. Alternate maximum weights are placarded on the flight deck.

Aircraft General (AFM)

Configuration Deviation List (CDL):
When operation is scheduled with certain secondary airframe and engine parts missing: The airplane must be operated in accordance with the CDL certificate limitations contained in the CDL section of the Minimum Equipment List Manual

Passenger Evacuation Arming Requirements
Prior to Taxi, Takeoff and Landing whenever passengers are carried:
- Main door emergency power assist systems and emergency evacuation slide systems must be armed with Mode Select Handles in the ARMED position.
- Girt bar indication flags are visible through windows in the doorway liners when the doors and slides are in the ARMED mode.

Cabin Phone Handsets: Must be stowed

Cabin Viewing Requirements:
- Passenger seat headrests must be lowered
- Partition viewing window must be opened

Flight Deck Security Door (AFM)   Preflight: Verify operational check has been accomplished according to approved procedures once each flight day

Overhead Flight Crew Rest (OFCR) Area and Overhead Flight Attendant Rest (OFAR) Area (AFM) 300ER: OFCR and OFAR are to be occupied by crew members only if they have been trained in use of the crew rest evacuation routes, firefighting procedures and depressurization procedures.

Broadband Comm Switch (AFM) Use during Deice: Must be **OFF** during deice operations on ground.

Oxygen Bottle Minimum Pressure
ETOPS: 1250 psi at 70°F
Non-ETOPS: 800 psi at 70°F · OMV1, Pre-Flight 10.13

Tire Pressure Minimums
Nose Gear: 190 psi
Main Gear: 200 psi · OMV1, Pre-Flight 10.13

WLAN · Cockpit Use: Prohibited on **200ER** two-class configuration

Air Systems (AFM)

Cabin Pressurization (AFM)
Maximum Cabin Pressure (Relief Valve): 9.1 psi
Maximum Cabin Pressure Differential for
Takeoff and Landing: 0.11 psi

APU to Pack Operation **300ER**: APU to Pack takeoffs prohibited at airport altitudes > 6900' field elevation

Anti-Ice, Rain (AFM)

Anti Ice Operations with Primary Ice
Detection System Inop:
- Do not rely on airframe visual cues to turn engine anti-ice on.
- Use temperature and visual moisture criteria as defined above.
- Delaying use of engine anti-icing until ice buildup is visible from cockpit may result in severe engine damage and/or flameout.

Upper Wing Surface Check for Cold Soaked Wing
Cold soaked wing should be suspected if: Frost or ice is observed on wing underside during walk around, **and**
A large amount of fuel was remaining in wing tanks after landing
(Frost on bottom of wing surface is allowed in that situation)
If suspected, may be checked from: Cabin windows
Allowable underwing frost with cold fuel: ⅛ Inch · OMV1, Systems 86.15

Engine Anti-Ice
Ground: Must be ON if icing conditions exist or are anticipated
Flight: Must be ON or AUTO if icing conditions exist or are anticipated
Exception In Flight: OAT Temperature is below -40°C (SAT).
Do Not Use Anti Ice When: OAT or TAT exceeds 10°C (50°F)

Icing Conditions Definition:
- OAT/TAT 10°C (50°F) **and**
- Visible moisture in any form is present (clouds, fog with visibility one mile or less, rain, snow, sleet, or ice crystals.)

In Addition, During Ground Ops and Takeoff: When operating on ramps, taxiways, or runways where surface snow, ice, standing water, or slush may be ingested by engines, or freeze on the engines, nacelles, or engine sensor probes.

And in Addition, In Flight: When indicated by the primary ice detection system.

Automatic Flight

Autopilot / Flight Director System
Minimum Altitudes for Autopilot Use (AFM)
Takeoff: 200 Feet AFL
Coupled to ILS Glideslope and localizer
LAND 2 or LAND 3 Annunciated: None
Without LAND 2 or LAND 3 Annunciated: 200 Feet AFL
Go Around Mode: None

One Engine Inoperative Min Engagement Altitude: 200' AGL · QRH, MANEUVERS 1.23
Aileron Trim Use with Autopilot Engaged: Prohibited
Automatic Approach with Flaps 25 (AFM): Category II and Category III operations & autoland **not** approved
Non-AFM Operational Information Do not use FLCH on final approach below 1000' AFE
Automatic landings

Flap Settings **May** be made with flaps: 20 or 30
Engines Single or dual engine Operation: Both operating **OR** one engine inoperative
Annunciator Autopilot Flight Director System
(AFDS) Autoland Status Annunciation: Must display **LAND 2** or **LAND 3**
May NOT be Made with **EICAS**: These messages, if displayed, prohibit automatic landings:
- SLATS DRIVE (AFM)
- PITCH UP AUTHORITY

Wind: See Operational Limitations Section, *page 6* of this book.
Glideslope Angle (AFM) Maximum angle: 3.25°
Minimum angle: 2.5°
Overweight Autoland **not** recommended · OMV1, APP-LDG-G/A 45.23

Communications (AFM)

Boom Microphones (not AFM)	If Operative:	Must be used below 18,000 Feet
HF Radios	Prohibited Use HF Frequencies:	♦ 11.133 MHz ♦ 22.683 MHz ♦ 29.489 MHz ♦ 22.434 MHz ♦ 22.766 MHz ♦ 29.490 MHz
	Use of One HF radio for Transmission:	Deselect other HF radio on all audio select panels (prevents audio interference)

Engines, APU

		300ER	**200ER**
Reverse Thrust	Ground:	Use for ground operation only	
			After a rejected takeoff (RTO) deploying thrust reversers, takeoff prohibited until maintenance complete.
	Thrust lever movement from reverse to forward:	Position thrust reverse levers full down (forward thrust) only after engines have decelerated to reverse idle	
	In-flight:	Intentional selection of reverse thrust in flight is prohibited	
	Powerbacks:	Backing the airplane with use of reverse thrust is prohibited	

APU Starter Duty Cycle (Not AFM)

	Maximum Start Attempts Within 60 Minutes:	Three attempts maximum	
		Electric Starter Motor Wait:	**For Turbine Starter Wait:**
	Between 1 & 2:	1 Minute	1 Minute
	Between 2 & 3:	1 Minute	1 Minute
	Thrust lever movement from reverse to forward:	Position thrust reverse levers full down (forward thrust) only after engines have decelerated to reverse idle	
	In-flight:	Intentional selection of reverse thrust in flight is prohibited	
	Powerbacks:	Backing the airplane with use of reverse thrust is prohibited	

Engine Starter	Starter Motor Operation:	**300ER**	**200ER**
		Up to 5 minutes (max) on, followed by 10 minutes off followed by 5 minutes (max) on Then allow to cool for 10 minutes before subsequent operation	Up to 3 minutes continuous operation then run down to 10% N3, followed by: A further 3 minutes continuous operation then run down to zero N3, followed by: Up to 1 minute continuous operation then run down to zero N3 and allow to cool for 30 minutes. _OR_ Above operating procedures can be replaced by: Up to 6 1/2 minutes continuous operation then run down to zero N3 and allow to cool for 30 minutes.

OMV1, STARTING 15.3

Maximum Autostart Cycles:	Autostart system may initiate a second auto-initiated attempt (**200**) or third attempt (**300**) No AML entry unless EICAS message is generated as a result of a failed autostart

OMV1, STARTING 15.1

Engine Limit Display Markings (AFM)

Maximum and Minimum Limits:	RED
Cautionary Limits:	AMBER
Ground Operation in Icing Conditions Run Up:	During ground operations (including taxi-in and taxi-out) in icing when the OAT is 3°C or below, the engine must be run up momentarily to a minimum of 50% N1 at intervals not to exceed 60 minutes.

		300ER	**200ER**
Maximum RPM	N1:	110.5%	100.5%
	N2:	121%	105.0%
	N3:		102.5%
Maximum EGT	Starting:	750° (Ground, No time limit) 825° (Inflight, No time limit)	700° (Momentary)
	Flight:	**17,000' and below** 1095°.................30 Seconds **All Altitudes** 1050°................No time limit 1090°C...............5 minutes	**Takeoff** 920°......................20 Seconds 900°.........................5 Minutes **Max Continuous Thrust** 850°C................No time limit

Note: *Removed from OMV1 Limitations. To be added to future OMV2 revision*

Oil System

Quantity (Not AFM Limits)	Minimum prior to engine start ....21 quarts	Minimum prior to engine start ....16 Quarts

LIMITATIONS section and OMV1, SYSTEMS 45.6

	300ER	**200ER**
Post-flight — Contact maintenance if below:	22 Quarts	18 Quarts
		OMV1, After Landing—Parking 15.2
Pressure — Minimum at Idle RPM:	Oil Pressure Minimum ....10 psi **Note:** *Temporary operation below 10 psi during negative G operation is limited to 15 seconds maximum.*	Idle Minimum ....25 psi Minimum at max continuous thrust ....50 psi
Temperature — Minimum:		Minimum for Engine Start ...-40°C Minimum for Advancing Thrust Levers to Takeoff Power..50°C
Maximum for Continuous Operation: for 15 Minute Limit:	132°C 143°C	191°C Not Specified

Ground Operation in Freezing Fog **200ER**
(AD 2008-02-05)   Visibility < 300m (985')
and OAT 0 to -6°C:
or OAT -7 to -13°C *and* taxi time > 45 minutes:
or OAT < -13°C *and* taxi time > 45 minutes:
Any temperature, if takeoff within
60 minutes total taxi time:

Run up engines to 50% N1 for 1 minute every 45 minutes taxi time
Run up the engines to 59% N1 for 1 minute every 45 minutes taxi time
No run-up procedure; the engines must be manually de-iced.

Regardless of temperature, if the core ice shedding procedure described above is not accomplished within 45 minutes total taxi time in freezing fog with visibility 300 meters (985 feet) or less, but takeoff can be achieved within 60 minutes total taxi time in freezing fog with visibility of 300 meters (985 feet) or less,
♦ Takeoff is permitted.
♦ A borescope inspection is required within 10 flights.

If total taxi time in freezing fog with visibility of 300 meters (985 feet) or less exceeds 60 minutes without accomplishing ice shed the above core procedure:

♦ Takeoff is not permitted.
♦ The engine core must be manually de-iced.

Single Engine Taxi — Not Authorized when:
(WIT)

*W*et or slippery taxiways
*I*cy conditions
*T*ight turns/confined areas expected
300ER (always)   OMV1, TAXI-TAKEOFF 10.4

Not Recommended for:
APU Use: Not required for SE taxi   OMV1, TAXI-TAKEOFF 10.4
Reversers — Inspection Requirement: **200** Following any rejected takeoff in which thrust reverser(s) were deployed, maintenance must *determine* if an inspection is required *prior to subsequent takeoff*.   See QRH Maneuvers-1.12
                                                                                                    QRH Landing Gear 14.5

Flight Controls (AFM)

Flight Controls, General — Manual Inputs: Avoid rapid and large alternating control inputs, especially in combination with large changes in pitch, roll, or yaw (e.g. large side slip angles) as they may result in structural failure at any speed, including below V_A.

Flight Control Mode (AFM) — Authorized T/O Mode: Takeoff is permitted only in the **NORMAL** flight control mode

Flight Instruments

RVSM Operations — Altimeter Tolerances: CA & FO Altimeters must agree with field elevation ☐75 feet
Standby Altimeter & RVSM   STBY Altimeter does not meet RVSM accuracy requirements.
Difference between CA & F/O Altitude Displays: 200' maximum allowable for RVSM operations
Ground Maneuver Camera System **300ER**   Use: Should not be used during takeoff approach, and landing
RNAV (RNP) Minimum Required Navigation Performance   Note: *To get to / change RNP in FMC:*
(RNP) — RNAV (RNP) Approaches: ≤0.3 NM (or as published)   *Select CDU PROG page, then button 6R*
For RNAV (RNP) Missed Approaches: No Restriction   Reference: OMV1,
Maximum Speed on Final Approach Segment: 180 Knots   APPROACH LANDING GO-AROUND-25.4
Minimum RNAV RNP Authorized: 0.11 NM   APPROACH LANDING GO-AROUND-25.11

FMS

Air Data Inertial Reference Unit (ADIRU) (AFM)
Alignment Locations: ADIRU Alignment must not be attempted at latitudes greater than 78°, 14.75 minutes
QFE Altimeter Use   Not authorized (QNH required).
RNAV Use for SIDs and STARs — Building: May not be built—must be loaded from current NAV data base.
Do Not Accept RNAV SID Clearance if: ♦ Runway position, identification, or lateral track depiction on ND is inaccurate
♦ NAV UNABLE RNP EICAS message is displayed
♦ There is a loss of FMS or lateral navigation flight mode guidance (flight director and/or LNAV mode inoperative)
                                                                            OMV1, TAXI-TAKEOFF-20.11

Holding—Maximum Speed — <6000':   200 KIAS
>6000 through 14,000':   230 KIAS   ♦*May be restricted to 210 when on a low altitude chart*
                                                ♦*If 210 must be exceeded in this case, notify ATC*
>14,000':   265 KIAS   FOM Gen Ops > International > Maximum Holding Speeds1i-20

Fuel (AFM)

Types of Fuels	Approved for Use:	Jet A, Jet A-1, JP-5, and JP-8
	Prohibited Fuels:	JP-4 and Jet B
	Other Fuel Usage:	Must be coordinated with MOC (Not an AFM)
Fuel Tank Temperature Minimum	Prior to Takeoff:	Must not be less than the greater of
		♦ -40°C, **OR**
		♦ 3°C above the freezing point of the fuel being used
	In Flight:	Must be maintained at least 3°C above the freezing point of the fuel being used
	Use of Fuel System Icing Inhibitor Additives:	Do not change the minimum fuel tank temperature limit.
Fuel Tank Temperature Maximum		49°C (120°F)

		300ER	**200ER**
Usable Fuel Tank Max Quantities	Main L or R:	69,000 lbs	64,100 lbs
	Center:	182,800 lbs	174,900 lbs

1. *Based on density of 6.7 lbs. per gallon.*
2. *Total fuel at standard density is* **300ER** *320,800;* **200ER** *303,100 lbs.*

Density	Must be between:	6.1 and 7.1 pounds per gallon
Fuel Loading	Order of Fueling:	♦ Tanks may be loaded individually, simultaneously, or in any sequence
		♦ Main Tanks must be loaded equally to the desired fuel quantity or until full

Center Tank — If Loading Fuel in Center Tank: Main tanks must be *scheduled* to be full

Note: *Center tank may contain up to 3,000 pounds of fuel with less than full main tanks provided the weight of the fuel in the center tank plus the actual zero fuel weight does not exceed the Maximum Zero Fuel Weight, and the Center of Gravity limits are observed.*

Fuel Usage	Minimum Fuel Crossfeed Valve Use:	For minimum fuel operation, a crossfeed valve is opened.
	Correcting Fuel Imbalance:	Open a crossfeed valve and turn off the Fuel Pump Switches for the fuel tank that has the lowest quantity.

Fuel Imbalance Between Main Tanks, for Taxi, Takeoff and Landing With Main Tank Fuel

> 123,000 **300ER** or 114,000 **200ER** lbs:	3,000 pounds	*Average— 61,500* **300ER**, *57,000* **200ER** *lbs per tank.*
< 90,000 **300ER** or 50,000 **200ER** lbs:	4,500 pounds	*Average— 45,000* **300ER**, *25,000* **200ER** *lbs per tank.*
Between ranges above for **300ER** or **200ER** respectively:	Linear interpolation between 3,000 and 4,500 pounds.	
Refueling During Refueling, Do Not Operate:	HF radios. (Not AFM)	

Warning Systems (AFM)

Ground Proximity Warning System (GPWS)
Look-Ahead Terrain Alerting (AFM)

Use for Navigation:	Not Allowed
Use of Look-Ahead Terrain Alerting and Terrain Display Functions are Prohibited:	Within 15 NM of takeoff, approach or landing at an airport or runway not contained in the GPWS terrain database

Note: *All AA authorized airports (Regular, provisional, refueling, alternate and designated) are contained in the GPS airport database.*

TCAS (AFM)	Deviation Authorization:	Pilots are authorized to deviate from their current ATC clearance to the extent necessary to comply with a TCAS RA
Weather Radar	Avoid operation:	♦ In a hangar
		♦ Within 50 feet of fueling operation of a fuel spill (not an AFM)
		♦ With personnel within the area normally enclosed by the radome

Note: *Does not apply to the weather radar* **TEST** *mode.*

Emergencies

Former Memory Items have been removed from required study.
They are included here for awareness only.

Cabin Altitude (2.1)
Condition: A cabin altitude is excessive.

1 Don the oxygen masks.
2 Establish crew communications.
3 Check the cabin altitude and rate.
4 **If** the cabin altitude is uncontrollable:
PASS OXYGEN switch......Push to ON and hold for 1 second
Without Delay:
Emergency descent accomplish.

- -

Aborted Engine Start L, R (7.1)
Condition: On the ground, an aborted engine start is needed.

FUEL CONTROL switch (affected side) ....
CUTOFF

- -

Dual Engine Failure / Stall (7.2) 300ER)
(7.4) 200ER)
Condition: Engine speed for both engines is below idle.

1 FUEL CONTROL switches (both)..............CUTOFF, then RUN
2 RAM AIR TURBINE switch ....Push and hold for 1 second

- -

Engine Autostart L, R (7.5) 300ER)
(7.6) 200ER)

Condition: During a ground start, one of these occurs:
• Autostart did not start the engine
• Fuel control switch is in RUN at low engine RPM with the autostart switch off

1 FUEL CONTROL switch (affected side) ....
CUTOFF

- -

Engine Lim/Surge/Stall L,R (7.7)
Condition: One or more of these occur:
• Engine indications are abnormal
• Engine indications are quickly nearing or show an exceedance
• Abnormal engine noises are heard, possibly with airframe vibration
• There is no response to thrust lever movement or the response is abnormal.
• Flames in the engine inlet or exhaust are reported

1 A/T ARM switch (affected side) ....Confirm ....OFF
2 Thrust Lever (affected side) ....Confirm............Retard until engine indications stay within limits or the thrust lever is at idle

- -

Engine Severe Damage/Separation L,R (7.10)
Condition: One or more of these occur:
• Airframe vibration with abnormal engine indications
• Engine separation.

1 A/T ARM switch (affected side).................Confirm............OFF
2 Thrust Lever (affected side) ....Confirm............Idle
3 FUEL CONTROL switch (affected side) ....Confirm ....CUTOFF
4 Engine fire switch (affected side).............Confirm ....Pull

- -

Fire Engine L,R (8.2)
Condition: Fire is detected in the engine.

1 A/T ARM switch (affected side).................Confirm............OFF
2 Thrust Lever (affected side) ....Confirm............Idle
3 FUEL CONTROL switch (affected side) ....Confirm ....CUTOFF
4 Engine fire switch (affected side).............Confirm ....Pull
5 **If** the FIRE ENG message stays shown:
Engine fire switch (affected side)........................Rotate to the stop and hold for 1 second

⚠ ⎡ **If on the ground, do NOT wait 30 seconds.**
If after 30 seconds, the FIRE ENG message stays shown:
Engine fire switch (affected side) ....Rotate to the other stop and hold for 1 second

- -

Stabilizer (9.1)
Condition: One of these occurs:
• Stabilizer movement without a signal to trim
• The stabilizer is failed.

1 Stab cutout switches (both)..CUTOUT
....................Do not exceed the current airspeed.

- -

Airspeed Unreliable (10.1)
Condition: The airspeed or Mach indications are suspected to be unreliable. (Items which may indicate unreliable airspeed are listed in Supplemental Information at the end of this checklist.)
Objective: To identify a reliable airspeed indication if possible, or to continue the flight using the Flight with Unreliable Airspeed tables following this checklist.

1 Autopilot disengage switch ....Push
2 A/T ARM switches (both) ....OFF
3 F/D switches (both) ....OFF
4 Set the following gear up pitch attitude and thrust:
Flaps extended ....10 Degrees and 85% N1
Flaps Up   4 degrees and 70% N1

Note: *Only selected maneuvers are reproduced here for study. Notes are abbreviated for brevity and ease of study. Refer to QRH, MANEUVERS section for other procedures and full text of notes. Procedures are taken from the QRH, which states, "**This section is a consolidation of emergency maneuvers. Pilots are expected to be proficient in the performance of these maneuvers.**"*

Approach to Stall or Stall Recovery

All recoveries from approach to stall should be done as if an actual stall has occurred. Immediately do the following at the first indication of stall (buffet or stick shaker).

Reduction of angle of attack is the most important action to recovery from an impending stall or full stall.

WARNING
*Excessive use of pitch trim or rudder may aggravate the condition, or may result in loss of control or in high structural loads.

NOTE
Do not use flight director commands during the recovery. If autopilot response is not acceptable, it should be disengaged. If autothrottle response is not acceptable, it should be disconnected.

NOTE
If autopilot response is not acceptable, it should be disengaged. If autothrottle response is not acceptable, it should be disconnected.

(OMV1, MANEUVERS 10.1.1):

Pilot Flying	Pilot Monitoring
Recognize and confirm the developing situation.	
First indication of stall (buffet or stick shaker)	
"My aircraft."	
Initiate the recovery: — Smoothly apply nose down elevator to reduce the angle of attack until buffet or stick shaker stops. Nose down stabilizer trim may be needed.*	Monitor altitude and airspeed Verify all required actions have been done
Continue the recovery: — Roll in the shortest direction to wings level if needed** — Advance thrust levers as needed — Retract the speedbrakes — Do not change gear or flap configuration, except • During liftoff, if flaps are up, call for flaps 1	Call out — Any omissions — Trend toward terrain contact Set the FLAP lever as directed
Complete the recovery: — Check airspeed and adjust thrust as needed — Establish pitch attitude — Return to the desired flight path Re-engage the autopilot and autothrottle if desired	Monitor altitude and airspeed Verify all required actions have been completed Call out — Any omissions — Trend toward terrain contact

Emergency Descent

CAUTION
Plan descent to remain above highest area terrain while altering flight path as needed for continued descent to 10,000 feet within PAX O2 time limits. Recommended high terrain descent profiles below may be adjusted as necessary to meet terrain clearance/PAX O2 requirements:

200ER PAX O2 12 Mins

Level Off at 17,000 feet for 10 minutes (or until terrain clearance is assured) from the time passenger oxygen was deployed, then descend to 10,000 feet or below.

300ER PAX O2 22 Mins

Level Off at 25,000 feet for 19 minutes (or until terrain clearance is assured) from the time passenger oxygen was deployed, then descend to 10,000 feet or below.

If temperatures are colder than ISA, the altimeter will indicate higher than the actual altitude. The error may be significant and becomes extremely important when considering obstacle clearances in very cold temperatures.

In extremely cold weather conditions (approximately -30°C SAT and below), add 2000 feet to the initial level-off altitude until safe terrain separation is ensured.

(OMV1, Maneuvers 10.2)
Also in Electronic checklist, Unannunciated Checklists

MCP Altitude ....Select lower
> **Note:** If due to depressurization, where passenger oxygen has been actuated, plan to reach 10,000 feet within passenger oxygen time limits and continue flight at 10,000 feet or below, unless operational or terrain considerations dictate otherwise.

FLCH ....Select
Thrust Levers ....Close
Speedbrake handle..Full aft
SEAT BELTS selector..ON
Descend..................Straight ahead or initiate moderate bank (30° max)
CAUTION
If structural integrity is in doubt, limit airspeed and avoid high maneuvering loads.

Target speed ....Max VMO / MMO
Transponder...Code 7700
> (Unless voice communications with ATC are established.)

ATC..Call
Make PA ....Use oxygen – fasten seat belts
> Advise Flight Attendants, via PA, when they can remove their oxygen masks (cabin altitude at or below 10,000 feet).

Approaching Level Off Altitude (1000 feet above):
Speedbrakes..Retract

Note
If depressurization has occurred and passenger oxygen has actuated, plan to reach 10,000 feet within passenger oxygen time limits and continue flight at 10,000 feet or below, unless operational or terrain considerations dictate otherwise.

Engine Failure on Final Approach
(Maneuvers 10.3)

See notes, Maneuver section of OMV1

Ground Proximity WARNING Actions & Callouts

200ER – activation of the "PULL UP", or "TERRAIN TERRAIN PULL UP" warning

300ER – activation of the "PULL UP", or "OBSTACLE OBSTACLE PULL UP", or "TERRAIN TERRAIN PULL UP" warning
Other situations resulting in unacceptable flight toward terrain

Note
Aft control column force increases as the airspeed decreases. In all cases, the pitch attitude that results in intermittent stick shaker or initial buffet is the upper pitch attitude limit. Flight at intermittent stick shaker may be required to obtain positive terrain separation. Smooth, steady control will avoid a pitch attitude overshoot and stall.

Do not use flight director commands.

If positive visual verification is made that no obstacle or terrain hazard exists when flying under daylight VMC conditions prior to an obstacle or terrain warning, the alert may be regarded as cautionary and the approach may be continued.

(OMV1, MANEUVERS 10.4.1)

Pilot Flying	Pilot Monitoring
Ground proximity *warning* alert	
"My aircraft."	
Immediately and simultaneously: — Disengage autopilot — Disconnect autothrottles — Aggressively apply maximum* thrust — Simultaneously roll wings level and rotate to an initial pitch attitude of 20° — Retract speedbrakes — If terrain remains a threat, continue rotation up to the pitch limit indicator or stick shaker or initial buffet — Do not change gear or flap configuration until terrain separation is assured — Monitor radio altimeter for sustained or increasing terrain separation — When clear of the terrain, slowly decrease pitch attitude and accelerate	— Assure maximum* thrust — Verify all required actions have been completed Call out any omissions Monitor vertical speed and altitude (radio altitude for terrain clearance and barometric altitude for a minimum safe altitude) Call out: — Any omissions — Any trend toward terrain contact ### Note * Maximum thrust can be obtained by advancing the thrust levers to the takeoff or go-around limit. On aircraft with EECs operating normally, the pilot may advance the thrust levers full forward. If terrain contact is imminent, advance thrust levers full forward.

Ground Proximity **CAUTION** Actions & Callouts	Pilot Flying	Pilot Monitoring
300ER Accomplish the following maneuver for any of these aural alerts:	Ground proximity *caution* aural alert activated	
— CAUTION OBSTACLE — SINK RATE — CAUTION TERRAIN — TOO LOW FLAPS — TERRAIN — TOO LOW GEAR — DON'T SINK — TOO LOW TERRAIN — GLIDESLOPE — BANK ANGLE	Correct the flight path or the aircraft configuration	
(OMV1, MANEUVERS 10.4.2)	**Note** If a terrain caution occurs when flying under daylight VMC, and positive visual verification is made that no obstacle or terrain hazard exists, the alert may be regarded as cautionary and the approach may be continued.	

Moderate to Severe Turbulence Encounter

Speed..Turbulent Air Penetration
- 270 KIAS below 25,000 feet
- 280 KIAS/.82 Mach (whichever is lower) at and above 25,000 feet. Maintain a minimum speed of 15 knots above the minimum maneuvering speed (amber band) at all altitudes when the airspeed is below 0.82 Mach

Flap extension.................................Delay as long as possible
The aircraft can withstand higher gust loads in the clean configuration

Seat Belt Signs selector ....ON

Make PA
Refer to Flight Manual Pt 1 - Section 11 - Non-Routine PAs Typical Examples - Turbulence.

Autothrottles..As required
In severe turbulence during cruise, it may be necessary to disconnect the autothrottles to prevent excessive thrust changes. Thrust setting guidance is available on EICAS when VNAV is engaged. Set EPR/N1 at or slightly above the magenta VNAV target EPR/N1 indication. Change thrust setting only if required to modify an unacceptable speed trend.

Autopilot..Monitor
Use the autopilot in turbulence. Closely monitor autopilot operation and be prepared to disconnect the autopilot only if the aircraft does not maintain an acceptable attitude. If the autopilot disconnects, the pilot should smoothly take control and stabilize the pitch attitude.

(OMV1, Maneuvers 10.5.1)

Rejected Takeoff
After RTO Considerations

When stopped. perform procedures as required.

<u>Prior to 80 knots</u>, the takeoff should be rejected for any of the following:
- Activation of the master caution system
- System failure(s)
- Unusual noise or vibration
- Tire failure
- Abnormally slow acceleration
- Takeoff configuration warning
- Fire or fire warning
- Engine failure
- Predictive windshear warning
- If a side window opens
- If the aircraft is unsafe or unable to fly

<u>Above 80 knots and prior to V1</u>, the takeoff should be rejected for any of the following:
- Fire or fire warning
- Engine failure
- Predictive windshear warning or caution
- If the aircraft is unsafe or unable to fly

During the takeoff, the crewmember observing the non-normal situation will immediately call it out as clearly as possible.

See additional notes in QRH.

Note

If an engine failure occurs above TAC activation speed, TAC provides a rudder input, as needed, to help maintain directional control. TAC rudder input is available during forward thrust operations only, until speed is reduced below TAC activation speed. With TAC inoperative, the PF must make rudder inputs.

(OMV1, MANEUVERS 10.6.1)

Captain	First Officer
The captain decides to reject the takeoff	
"Reject, my aircraft."	
	If aircraft control is transferred
	"Your aircraft."
Immediately and simultaneously: — Close the thrust levers — Disengage the autothrottle — Apply maximum manual wheel brakes or verify operation of RTO autobrakes. If RTO autobrakes is selected, monitor system performance and apply manual wheel brakes if the EICAS advisory message **AUTOBRAKE** displays or deceleration is not adequate — Apply reverse thrust up to the maximum amount consistent with conditions — If speedbrakes do not deploy (or fail to remain deployed), manually deploy speedbrakes — Continue maximum braking until certain the aircraft will stop on the runway.	Verify: — Thrust levers closed — Autothrottle disengaged — Maximum brakes applied
	If EICAS advisory message AUTOBRAKES displays during rollout
	"Autobrakes off."
	Verify SPEEDBRAKE lever full aft
	"Deployed." or If speedbrakes do not deploy (or fail to remain deployed **"No Speedbrakes"**
	If there is no REV indication(s) or the indication(s) stays amber
	"No reverser left engine." or **"No reverser right engine."** or **"No reversers."**
	Call out any omitted action items
	Apply forward pressure on the control column
At 80 knots	
	"80."
At 60 knots	
	"60."
When stopping is assured: — Start movement of the reverse thrust levers to reach the reverse idle detent before taxi speed. — After the engines are at reverse idle, mode the thrust levers to full down.	
Communicate the reject decision to the control tower and appropriate crew members as soon as practical — If needed, make PA, *"This is the captain. Remain seated. Remain seated. Remain seated."*	

Takeoff Engine Failure/Loss of Thrust After V₁ Actions & Callouts

See additional notes in QRH

[1] If the FD TAKEOFF mode is engaged at time of engine failure, the FD will command this speed schedule. However, do not follow the FD pitch command bar until safely airborne.
[2] Verify engine thrust is at takeoff thrust setting until aircraft is in clean configuration and obstacle clearance is assured.

(OMV1, MANEUVERS 10.7.1)

Pilot Flying	Pilot Monitoring
Engine failure or loss of thrust	
"My aircraft."	
Maintain directional control	
At V$_R$	
	"Rotate."
Rotate to takeoff attitude	
After liftoff	
Verify positive rate of climb on altimeter	Verify positive rate of climb on the altimeter
	"Positive Rate."
"Gear up."	On command, Landing Gear Lever
Use the following climb s Use the following climb speed to the TPS engine-out acceleration altitude: — **If engine failure occurs after V1, but not above V₂:** • Maintain minimum V₂ — **If engine failure occurs between V₂ and V₂ + 15:** • Maintain speed attained at time of failure — **If engine failure occurs at a speed greater than V₂ + 15:** • Increase pitch to reduce airspeed to V₂ + 15 [1]	Monitor engine and flight instruments [2]
At the TPS engine-out acceleration altitude	
Accelerate and command flap retraction on schedule	On command, retract flaps
Aircraft in clean configuration and VREF 30 + 80	
Call for the appropriate checklist(s)	
	Accomplish the appropriate checklist(s) on command

(Left side marking: 1 ENGINE)

Traffic Advisory (TA) Actions & Callouts

WARNING

Comply with RA if there is a conflict between RA and air traffic control.

Once an RA has been issued, safe separation can be compromised if current vertical speed is changed, except as necessary to comply with the RA. This is because TCAS II-to-TCAS II coordination may be in progress with the intruder aircraft, and any change in vertical speed that does not comply with the RA may negate the effectiveness of the other aircraft's compliance with the RA.

(OMV1, MANEUVERS 10.8.1)

Pilot Flying	Pilot Monitoring
TCAS traffic advisory (TA) occurs	
Look for traffic using traffic display as a guide	
Call out any conflicting traffic	
If traffic is sighted, maneuver if needed	

Note

See numerous additional notes in Operating Manual.

Resolution Advisory (RA) - Except a Climb in Landing Configuration Actions & Callouts

(OMV1, MANEUVERS 10.8.2)

Pilot Flying	Pilot Monitoring
TCAS resolution advisory (RA)	
"My aircraft."	
— If maneuvering is required, disengage the autopilot and disconnect the autothrottles — Smoothly adjust pitch and thrust to satisfy the RA command — Follow the planned lateral flight path unless visual contact with the conflicting traffic requires other action	
Attempt to establish visual contact.	
Call out any conflicting traffic	

Climb RA in Landing Configuration Actions & Callouts

Note: When responding to an RA, the aircraft should be maneuvered only as much as needed to satisfy the RA.

(OMV1, MANEUVERS 10.8.3)

Captain	First Officer
TCAS resolution advisory (RA)	
"My aircraft."	
— Disengage autopilot — Disconnect autothrottle — Advance thrust levers forward to ensure maximum thrust is attained and call for FLAPS 20 — Smoothly adjust pitch to satisfy the RA command — Follow planned lateral flight path unless visual contact with conflicting traffic requires other action	— Verify maximum thrust set. — On command, position flap lever to 20 detent
Verify a positive rate of climb on the altimeter	Verify a positive rate of climb on the altimeter
	"Positive Rate"
"Gear Up."	On command, Landing Gear Lever **UP**
Attempt to establish visual contact	
Call out any conflicting traffic	

Upset Recovery
Nose High Recovery Actions & Callouts

WARNING

* Excessive use of pitch trim or rudder may aggravate an unusual attitude or may result in loss of control and/or high structural loads.

Pilot Flying	Pilot Monitoring
Recognize and confirm the developing situation	
First indication of nose high upset	
"My aircraft."	
— Disengage autopilot — Disconnect autothrottle — Apply as much as full nose down elevator — *Apply appropriate nose down stabilizer trim — Reduce thrust — *Roll (adjust bank angle) to obtain a nose down pitch rate — Complete the recovery: • When approaching the horizon, roll to wings level • Check airspeed and adjust thrust • Establish pitch attitude	Call out — Any omissions — Attitude, airspeed and altitude throughout the recovery
	Verify all required actions have been completed

(OMV1, MANEUVERS 10.9.1)

Upset Recovery
Nose Low Recovery Actions & Callouts

WARNING

* Excessive use of pitch trim or rudder can aggravate an upset, result in loss of control, or result in high structural loads.

Pilot Flying	Pilot Monitoring
Recognize and confirm the developing situation	
First indication of nose low upset	
"My aircraft."	
— Disengage autopilot — Disconnect autothrottle — Recover: • Recover from stall, if needed • Roll in the shortest direction to wings level (unload and roll if bank angle is more than 90°)* — Recover to level flight: • Apply nose up elevator • Apply nose up trim, if needed * • Adjust thrust and drag, if needed	Call out — Any omissions — Attitude, airspeed and altitude throughout the recovery
	Verify all required actions have been completed

(OMV1, MANEUVERS 10.9.2)

Windshear or Microburst Escape

[1] If go-around is not available, disconnect autopilot and autothrottle and manually fly the aircraft.
[2] Severe windshear may exceed the performance capability of the AFDS.
[3] Maximum thrust can be obtained by advancing the thrust levers full forward if the EECs are in the normal mode. If terrain contact is imminent, advance thrust levers full forward.

Pilot Flying		Pilot Monitoring
When encountering a windshear		
Call "Escape"		
"My aircraft."		
A u t o	— Push either TO/GA switch[1] — Ensure TO/GA mode annunciation and GA thrust — Monitor system performance **WARNING:** Be prepared to disconnect the autopilot and autothrottle and manually fly the aircraft.[2]	• Ensure all required actions are completed
M a n u a l	**Simultaneously:** — Disconnect the autopilot — Push either go-around switch — Aggressively apply maximum thrust[3]	Call out • any omissions • altitude and trend information based on radio altimeter (e.g., "300 feet descending" or "400 feet climbing")
	— Disconnect the autothrottle — Roll wings level and rotate toward an initial pitch attitude of 15° — Follow TO/GA guidance (if available) without exceeding pitch limit indication (PLI)	
Ensure the speed brakes are retracted		
Do not: • change gear/flap configuration • attempt to regain lost airspeed *until* windshear is no longer a factor		
After escape is successful		
• Resume normal flight • Retract gear and flaps as required		• Issue PIREP to ATC

(QRH Maneuvers 10.10.1)

Windshear Alerts: During Takeoff

[1] Inhibited from 80 knots to 400 feet RA.
[2] Inhibited from 100 knots to 50 feet RA.
[3] Inhibited until rotation.

(OMV1, MANEUVERS 10.10.2)

Alert	Prior to V1	At or Above V1
Caution[1] "Monitor radar display."	Delay/reject the takeoff	• Maneuver as required to avoid windshear • Use maximum thrust
Warning "Windshear ahead. Windshear ahead."[2] or "Windshear. Windshear. Windshear."[3]	Delay/reject the takeoff	Perform the Windshear Escape Maneuver
Unacceptable Flight Deviations	Reject the takeoff	• Perform the Windshear Escape Maneuver • At V_R, rotate normally to 15° no later than 2000 feet runway remaining

Windshear Alerts: During Approach

[1] **Inhibited below 400 feet RA.**
[2] Inhibited below 50 feet RA.

(OMV1, MANEUVERS 10.10.3)

Alert/Aural	During Approach
Caution[1] "Windshear." or "Monitor radar display."	— Execute a normal go-around and maneuver as necessary to avoid windshear **OR** — Continue the approach at captain's discretion if able to avoid windshear[1]
Warning[2] "Go around. Windshear ahead."	— Perform at pilot's discretion either: • A normal go-around or • The windshear escape maneuver
Warning "Windshear. Windshear. Windshear."	Perform the windshear escape maneuver
Unacceptable Flight Deviations	

Windshear Warning
(OMV1, MANEUVERS 10.10.4)

Pilot Flying	Pilot Monitoring
Maneuver as required to avoid windshear	

Predictive windshear warning during takeoff roll: ("WINDSHEAR AHEAD, WINDSHEAR AHEAD" aural)
— Prior to V1, reject takeoff
— After V1, perform the Windshear Escape Maneuver Windshear encountered during takeoff roll:
— If windshear is encountered prior to V1, there may not be sufficient runway remaining to stop if an RTO is initiated at V1. At Vr, rotate at a normal rate toward a 15° pitch attitude. Once airborne, perform the Windshear Escape Maneuver.
— If windshear is encountered near the normal rotation speed and airspeed suddenly decreases, there may not be sufficient runway left to accelerate back to normal takeoff speed. If there is insufficient runway left to stop, initiate a normal rotation at least 2000 feet before the end of the runway even if airspeed is low. Higher than normal attitudes may be required to lift off in the remaining runway. Ensure maximum thrust is set. Predictive windshear warning during approach: ("GO-AROUND, WINDSHEAR AHEAD" aural)
— Perform Windshear Escape Maneuver or, at pilot's discretion, perform a normal go around Windshear encountered inflight:
— Perform the Windshear Escape Maneuver

Note

The following are indications the aircraft is in windshear:
—Windshear warning (two-tone siren followed by **"WINDSHEAR, WINDSHEAR, WINDSHEAR"**) or
—Unacceptable flight path deviations

Severe Weather / Windshear Procedures.

1. **Follow standard operating procedures:**
   — **Takeoff:** Minimize pitch attitude reductions
   — **Approach:** Avoid large thrust reductions
   — Know normal attitude and performance
2. **If predictive W/S caution or warning is received:**
   — **Aligned** for takeoff: Delay takeoff
   — **Prior to V₁ :** Reject takeoff
   — **Above V₁ :** Perform W/S Escape Maneuver
3. **Predictive W/S warning is received during approach ("GO-AROUND, WINDSHEAR AHEAD" aural):**
   — **Perform** W/S Escape Maneuver or, at pilot's discretion, perform a normal go-around
4. **Windshear encountered inflight:**
   — **Perform** W/S Escape Maneuver
   — **Report** encounter

Normal Procedures Notes

Note: *This chapter contains notes and references to some of the more commonly needed numbers and page numbers buried throughout the normal procedures, abnormal and systems sections of OMV1, and some information from the Flight Training Manual. To the extent practical, it is organized in the order these items are encountered in a normal flight profile.*

Type Approach & OM Page Reference		Lowest Visibility	AFDS Status Annunciation	Alert Height Required	Baro/Radio Bug*	Unique Call-Outs
Visual	App-Landing-G/A 20.1	3 Miles	N/A		Radio—Zero / OFF	
Non-ILS	App-Landing-G/A 25.1	As Published	N/A		Baro—MDA as DA or DDA (MDA + 50')	
CAT I	App-Landing-G/A 35.3	½ Mile / RVR 1800'	N/A		Baro—DA	
CAT II—Always with DH App-Landing-G/A 40.5 Airports with 300M published Vis Req:		1600 (500m) / 1200 (350m) 1000	LAND 2 or LAND 3	No	Radio—DH	All CAT II and CAT III —"*300*", based on RA **At DH**, "*Minimums*," if voice callouts inop
CAT III	App-Landing-G/A 40.8	600 (175m)	LAND 2	No	Radio—50' DH	
			LAND 3	No DH: Yes* DH: No	Radio—0' Radio—DH	
CAT III	App-Landing-G/A 40.8	300 (75m)	LAND 3	No DH: Yes* DH: No	Radio—0' Radio—DH	

Climb Speeds
Use ECON Cost-Index derived speed or the following:

Altitude	Gross Weight	Speed
Below 10,000 ft	All Weights	250 kts
Above 10,000 ft		310 kts / .84 m

Approach Types
LAND 2 (Fail Passive)
Redundancy such that:
  Single fault cannot cause significant deviation from flight path
  Could be caused by single A/P inop
  In the case of a failure, this mode will
    Stabilize the flight path on the localizer and glide slope
    NOT flare and land properly
    Require a go-around if a failure is detected
  Cat II Authorized
  CAT IIIa Authorized with 50' DH
  CAT IIIb NOT Authorized
LAND 3 (Fail Operational)
Redundancy such that:
  Single fault cannot prevent the autopilot system from making an automatic landing
  Must be done with three A/Ps
  In the case of a failure, this mode will
    Stabilize the flight path on the localizer and glide slope
    Flare and land properly if the failure does not cause the LAND 3 status to change
    Require a go-around if a failure is detected
  Cat II, IIIa & IIIb Authorized

Final Approach Deviation Callouts
Category Criteria...................Callout
Airspeed.........................+10 / -5 knots*..............*Airspeed*
Rate of Descent........<2000'—More than 2000 fpm......*Sink Rate*
.................<1000'—More than 1000 fpm*.....*Sink Rate*
Glide Slope ....> ½ Dot Deviation.........*Glide Slope*
Localizer.......................> ⅓ Dot Deviation ....*Localizer*
Vertical Path Deviation........Call out any.....................*Path*
Lateral Track Deviation ....Call out any ....*Track*
VOR or NDB Deviation   Call out any.............*VOR* or *NDB*
Touchdown...First 1/3 of Runway Not to Exceed first 3000'*
* PNF directs GO AROUND if PF not correcting
APPROACH, LANDING, GO-AROUND 15.4-6

Autoland Requirement
For the **777 Fleet**, policy is that all CAT II and III approaches must end in
  Autolanding *OR*
  Go-Around
Manual landing is <u>not authorized</u> when below CAT I weather minimums

DH and AH
Not flown at the same time
DH requires external visual reference before passing specific altitude
AH does not have this visual requirement—only electronic verification

Lavatory and Water Systems
Water shutoffs
  Each lavatory has one behind mirror
    Mirror release button near wall under mirror
  Doors 2L and 4L have isolation zone shutoff valves
  Door 4L valve shuts off all water between doors 4 and 2
  Door 2L valve shuts off all water forward of doors 2L & R
  Aft Galley shutoff valve shuts off all water aft of doors 4L & R
Toilet Flush Shutoff
  Floor below toilet
  Can be used if toilet sticks in flush mode

Autobrakes
<u>Must be armed</u> (If operative) for any of the following:
◆ Runway length less than 7000 feet .... Setting 2 minimum
◆ RVR < 4000 or visibility < ¾ mile .... Setting 3 minimum
◆ Runway contaminated—standing water/snow/slush/ice
◆ Approach speed is increased above normal by procedure
◆ Braking conditions reported less than good
◆ CAT II and III landings ....Setting 3 minimum, if operable
◆ When minimum stopping distance is required ....Setting MAX
    Note *MAX Auto Brake deceleration is slightly less than full manual braking*
Recommended: landing with gusty winds or crosswinds
Recommended settings
  MAX AUTO—When minimum-stopping distance is required
    Deceleration rate is slightly less than that produced by full manual braking
  3 or 4—For wet / slippery runways or when landing rollout distance is limited
  2—For moderate deceleration
OMV1, APPROACH—LANDING—GO-AROUND 15.2, 25.11

Auto Speedbrake System
Will be armed for all landings (If operative)
Do not land with the Speedbrakes deployed
Use on Approach
  Use with flaps over 5 causes buffet
  Should be retracted by 1,000' AGL
OMV1, CLIMB-CRUSE-DESCENT 20.4
  Landing with thrust higher than idle may disable automatic deployment, causing a bounced landing
  If speedbrakes deploy and airplane becomes airborne again,
    They will retract while airborne
    Must then be manually redeployed
OMV1, APP-LDG-G/A 45.13
  If speedbrakes NOT raised after touchdown, braking effectiveness reduces by up to 60%
OMV1, APP-LDG-G/A 45.19

Takeoff Flap Selection

Authorized flap settings for takeoff are:
200ER aircraft with TO thrust ....Flaps 5, 15, & 20
200ER aircraft with TO1 or TO2 thrust.............Flaps 5 & 15
300ER aircraft with TO thrust......................Flaps 15 & 20
300ER aircraft with TO1 or TO2 thrust ....Flaps 15
Flaps 5, 15, & 20 are certified for takeoff on both aircraft, but not all combinations of flap setting / aircraft / thrust ratings are used by all operators.
Data for all of the authorized flap settings are not necessarily loaded in to TPS for all thrust ratings. Only data for the needed flap setting are loaded into TPS.
Contaminated Runway:
Flaps 15 (20 for **300ER**) recommended for takeoffs on contaminated runways to minimize the takeoff speeds.
If flaps 15 (20 for **300ER**) cannot be accommodated due to weight or conditions, coordinate another flap setting.

Landing Flap Selection

Use of flaps 25 is normally preferred:
♦ More fuel efficient
♦ Better noise abatement
♦ Reduced flap wear
♦ Improved maneuverability in high (gusty) wind conditions
Note: *The 777 is not certified for flaps 25 autoland.*
Use of flaps 30 is recommended when landing:
♦ Braking action reported less than good
♦ Tailwind
♦ Short runway (less than 8000 feet)
♦ Wet / contaminated runway
♦ When deemed prudent by the Captain
OMV1, APP-LDG-G/A 15.1

Approach Techniques

Initial Setup...**WARM**
Weather requirements..Check
Include crosswinds, visibility, published minimums
Approach............................Load Approach from Database
....Set minimums
....Brief Approach
RNP..As Required
MCP—When cleared for the approach ....LNAV / VNAV
....Set appropriate minimums when cleared for approach **and** on intercept heading **or** a portion of the approach
Captain Callouts......................................LOC / GS Intercept
....Passing FAF
Passing FAF Actions ....**MAC-V**
Missed approach Altitude ....Set when 300' below MAP
Altimeters—Verify CA—F/O.....................................± 100'
Clearance—Tower ....Call Passing FAF
V/S.......................Set prior to MDA if end point not RWXX
Note: *This section compiled from instructor notes and various OM references; NOT procedural, but technique recommendations.*

Briefings and Restrictions

Flight Attendant Briefing—Prior to gate departure

Known delays
Maintenance—cabin or galley writeup and deferrals in AML
Ground—Short-taxi & safety demo considerations
Crew
• Number of F/As onboard and minimum crew requirements
See paragraph 3g.10.2 Flight Attendants.
• Coordination of flightdeck crew meal service, if applicable
Time for meals is left to the CA's discretion
Cooperation should result in eating meals at desired time
• Need to minimize noise & activity near crew rest areas
Security
Details not included here for sensitivity concerns
Turbulence
• Weather/turbulence forecast for route: duration & severity
• Suspension of service at at flight attendant discretion
• Notification required action for unexpected turbulence
• Notify flightdeck of cabin situation & injuries if applicable
• If not seated at jumpseat with interphone, stay seated to avoid injury until instructed to resume duties by Captain
International
• Gen Decs/Customs Immigration forms (if required)
• N Atlantic flights north of 66°N over Greenland—request FA 1/purser review applicable FA Safety Manual information reference Supplemental O2 Unit ....FOM 3c.4.2

Use of Standard Thrust for takeoff is not authorized:

The following items require Maximum Takeoff Thrust at the TO rating:
♦ When using Improved Performance.
♦ If windshear is reported or expected.
♦ When Airport Ops Advisory (##-7) requires Maximum Thrust.
♦ When the runway is contaminated by standing water, slush, snow, or ice.
♦ Whenever takeoff data is used from the (Contaminated Runway Correction/MEL) CRC/MEL message for an MEL/ CDL item.
However, the following items require Maximum Takeoff Thrust, but may be used with any thrust rating (TO2, TO1, or TO):
♦ If Takeoff Weight (TOW) exceeds Assumed Takeoff Weight (ATOW). However, a new TPS may be obtained which authorizes Standard Thrust at the Takeoff Weight.
♦ With MEL / CDL items containing a takeoff weight correction UNLESS takeoff data is automatically corrected by TPS (TPAS), or MEL/CDL item prohibits standard thrust.
Performance Manual, TPS, Introduction 10.4

AC to Pack Takeoff **300ER**

Uses APU air to supply the left A/C pack
Use takeoff performance data based on A/C OFF
Applies to max weight, thrust, V-speeds, and assumed temperature......................................PERF TPS 10.6

Restricted Captain Requirements

Applies if
CA has < 100 hours after IOE in current aircraft type
Required 100 hours PIC in aircraft type may be reduced not to exceed 50% by substituting one landing for one hour of PIC time in aircraft type.
Restrictions _unless_ FAA Exemption 5549 apply
♦ Chart increases required visibility...................FOM, 18-45
♦ Alternate Airport - Published minima need not be increased, but lowest allowable landing minima is 300 feet MDA/DH and one mile visibility or 4500 RVR / 1400 meters
Practical Effect of Exemption 5549:
Recognizes inherent safety of autopilot coupled approaches
Allows approaches using
♦CAT II procedures to no lower CAT published minima or
♦CAT I procedures to published CAT I MDA, no lower than RVR 1800'
See detailed charts ....FOM, 18-45

Low Experience FO: <100 Hours (FAR 121.438)

When Applies—FO has **<100 hours** flight time as SIC in type aircraft being flown, **_and_**
Captain (PIC) is not a qualified Check Airman,
PIC must make all takeoffs when:
All special requirement airports
Visibility in the latest WX report at or below 3/4 mile
RVR for the runway to be used is at or below 4000 feet
Runway has water, snow, slush, or similar conditions which may adversely affect A/C performance
Braking action is reported less than good
Crosswind component >15kts
Windshear reported in the vicinity of the airport
Any other condition PIC determines prudent ....FOM, 18-46

Flight Attendants—Emergency TEST Acronym

Use only if evacuation is anticipated
T - Type of emergency; general description of the emergency
E - Evacuation is anticipated
S - Signal: the following PA:
"This is the Captain. Evacuate. Evacuate. Evacuate."
Followed by turning on Evacuation **COMMAND**.
T - Time: time to landing. ....QRH MISCELLANEOUS 0.24
See additional considerations regarding emergency evacuation in FOM..................................FOM, 1N.6.3 Evacuation

Emergency PA to Passengers

Nature of emergency
Time to landing
Passenger cooperation with Flight Attendants
Reassure passengers. ....QRH MISCELLANEOUS 0.25

Cold Weather Operations

Cold Weather Operations Ref ....OMV1, GENERAL 86.3 to 86.14

Icing Definition—Ground or Flight

OAT(Gnd) or TAT (Flt) < 10°C/50°F
AND Visible moisture present such as clouds, fog with visibility one mile or less, rain, snow, sleet, or ice crystals.
OR (Ground only) Temperature as above and
Any form of moisture is present (standing water, snow, slush etc.) *which may be*
Ingested by the engines and freeze on engine inlets, nacelles or engine sensor probes

In Flight Use
Engine anti-ice must be **AUTO** or **ON** during all flight operations when icing conditions exist or are anticipated, except when the temperature is below-40°C OAT (SAT)
CAUTION: *Do not use engine anti-ice when TAT is above 10°C.*

Preflight

<u>Advise Dispatch</u> if TPS adjustments needed for snow, slush ice or standing water
<u>Special Attention</u> for ice in:
♦ Wheel wells, actuators & steering components
♦ Flight controls (flaps, slats, control tabs, etc.)
♦ Wing surfaces (Max $1/8$ inch frost on bottom
♦ Pitot-Static components ♦ Engine Inlets
♦ Pack inlet/exit doors ♦ Fuel tank vents
♦ Pressure reg./relief valves ♦ APU Inlet
<u>Caution:</u> *Don't power up or move flight controls if ice could obstruct movement.*

Deicing

<u>Packs and Bleeds</u> (Engine & APU) OFF <u>During</u> and for 1 minute <u>after</u> deicing
<u>APU</u>--May be ON
<u>Engines</u> If operating, at idle power
<u>Before T/O Checklist</u> Must be completed in entirety following deicing

Lowest Operational Use Temperature (LOUT)
Defined as actual freeze point of a fluid plus additional fuel specific temperature buffer
See ....OMV1, General 20.16 and fuel holdover tables

Start/Taxi

<u>Caution:</u> *If frozen contamination in intakes, must be removed by certified deicing personnel.*
<u>Engine Start</u>—Ensure normal N_1 during start
Prohibited during pushback on slippery ramp surfaces
Captain can decide not to start until pushback complete in any icing conditions
<u>Oil Pressure</u> May be high due to low OAT
♦ Operate at idle until in normal range
♦ May use above idle for crossbleed start if req.
<u>Displays</u> may require additional warm up time or initially appear slightly dimmer than normal
<u>Engine Anti-Ice ON</u> Immediately after start if icing conditions exist or anticipated before T/O
<u>Flaps & Slats Up</u> until just before takeoff *if*
Taxi route is through ice, snow, slush or standing water or
Freezing precipitation continues after deice/anti-ice
<u>Flight Controls</u>—Check for *full travel* of <u>flight controls</u> and *free movement* of <u>trim</u>
<u>Run Engines Up</u> for approximately 1 second to 50% N_1
Applies when OAT is 3°C, 37°F or less and anti ice is required
Done at least once every 60 minutes
Reference OMV1, GENERAL 20.7
<u>Freezing Fog</u> Conditions (AD 2008-02-05)
Visibility less than 300 meters
Ice can build up on engine core
Shedding procedure—Momentary N1 run up to 50% every 45 minutes
Additional considerations: ....OMV1, Systems 86.3—86.4

Takeoff

If OAT is 3°C (37°F) or less static runup <u>required</u>
Minimum runup 50% N1
Confirm stable engine operation before starting takeoff roll
If runway contaminated, MAXIMUM thrust required

Climb, Cruise, Descent

Engine anti-ice must be AUTO or ON during all flight operations when
♦ Icing conditions exist or are anticipated, <u>except when</u>
♦ SAT is below-40°C OAT (SAT).
<u>Don't Operate Anti Ice</u> above 10° TAT
Fan Ice Removal
If moderate to severe icing conditions encountered for prolonged periods, <u>and</u>
Fan icing suspected due to high engine vibration,
Fan blades must be cleared of any ice.
300ER with N1 settings at or below 70%, every 15 minutes:
♦Reduce thrust toward idle, then
♦Increase to a minimum of 70% N1 for 10-30 seconds
200ER
♦Quickly reduce thrust to idle for 5 seconds then restore required thrust.
♦If vibration persists, advance thrust lever to 90% N1 momentarily ....OMV1 Systems 86.10—86.11
Wing anti ice use in flight
Required when structural icing is present
Indicated by ice build-up on
♦ Flight deck window frames ♦ Windshield wiper arm
♦ Windshield center post ♦ Side windows
<u>Primary method</u>—Use automatic ice detection system, which acts as a deicer and allows ice to build up before turning wing anti ice on
<u>Secondary method</u>—Select **WING ANTI ICE** selector **ON** when wing icing is possible and use as an anti-icer

Ice Crystal Icing

Threat to engines due to ice ingestion and damage
See definition and characteristics ....OMV1, Systems 86.11
Conducive condition recognition ....OMV1, CL-CR-DES 15.9
Prevention—Avoid flying directly over large convective cells with red radar returns, even if no returns at A/C Altitude
OMV1, CL-CR-DES 15.9-10

Landing

<u>Check Braking Conditions</u>—ATIS, Tower, etc.
<u>Runway Unfit for landing:</u>
♦ Pools of water, (accumulations of more than ½ inch)
♦ Wet snow, or slush (accumulations of more than ½ inch)
♦ Chunks of ice or hardened snow
♦ "Braking action NIL" is reported ....FOM 11g.2.2
<u>Slippery Runway Techniques</u>
♦ Land on speed
♦ Touchdown at planned point (Firm is better than "grease job" on icy runway)
♦ Nose--Keep firmly on runway with elevator
♦ Auto Brakes and Spoilers—Use
♦ Max Rev Thrust ASAP after touchdown *but*
-<u>Watch for asymmetric reverser</u> deployment
-<u>Avoid excessive reverse</u> on contaminated runway, which could lead to ice ingestion
-<u>Don't come out of reverse</u> at high RPM
♦ Use as much runway as needed to slow to taxi speed before turning off
<u>Visual Perception</u> problems possible with blowing snow—use caution

Taxi In & Parking

<u>Do not retract flaps if:</u>
Slush or Snow on runway *or*
Approach was in prolonged icing conditions
Call station for flap check, & deicing if req'd
<u>Call Dispatch</u>—Report runway as required
<u>Freezing Fog</u> Conditions (AD 2008-02-05)
Visibility less than 300 meters
Do run up momentary to 50% N1 within 5 minutes of parking aircraft in these conditions
<u>Braking Action Report</u> via ACARS
<u>if A/C is parked overnight in freezing temperatures:</u>
<u>Draining Water System</u> required
<u>Draining Lavatory Tanks</u> required unless anti-freeze is added
At off line stations with no AA maintenance, instructions available for station personnel or contract maintenance through Technical Services Group

Airplane General

Note: *This section contains notes on only selected "miscellaneous" components. They are the ones which, in the opinion of the author, are most necessary to know in time-critical situations.*

Lighting & Entertainment Systems

Passenger Cabin Signs

Fasten Seat Belt Signs—(10, 10, FOG)
In the **AUTO** position, on when:
- **10-A**ircraft below 10,000' MSL OR
- **10-C**abin pressure > 10,000' pressure alt. OR
- **F-F**lap handle not up OR
- **O-P**assenger Oxygen on OR
- **G-G**ear not up and locked

In the **OFF** position, FSB signs ON when
- **O-P**assenger Oxygen on

No Smoking Signs
On at all times
Chime sounds when moving switch between left and center positions
Chime *does not* sound when moving between center and right positions

Return to Seat Signs—Lavatories
ON whenever FSB signs are on *except*
OFF when passenger oxygen is deployed
Found in lavatories

300ER No Electronics Selector
OFF—ELECTRONIC DEVICES OFF (EDO) signs not illuminated
ON—EDO signs are **ON**
AUTO—EDO signs on when
- **G—**Ground; On ground, flaps not up, *or*
- **L—**Low Altitude; In flight, cabin altitude < 10,000', *or*
- **O—**Oxygen; Passenger oxygen on OMV2, 1.40.5

Note: *if used for chime before takeoff, must be cycled quickly (<1 second) to prevent activating PED video*

Emergency Lighting

Controlled <u>in cockpit</u> by overhead panel **EMER LIGHT** Switch
Automatic operation occurs when:
  System is armed *and*
    DC power fails or is turned off *or*
    An exterior door mode select lever is **ARMED** and the door is manually opened

In the latter case (door opened) exterior fuselage lighting at that door, and all interior emergency lighting comes on
Alternate control <u>in main cabin</u> on flight attendant panel at door 1L
Switch can be used to bypass cockpit switch
Will activate emergency lighting *regardless of the cockpit switch position*
EICAS **EMER LIGHTS** message is displayed if
Emergency lights switch is not in the armed position *or*
Emergency lights switch is armed, and the lighting is activated from the door 1L panel
Power for emergency lights
Remote batteries
Charged by airplane electrical system
Fully charged batteries provide at least 15 minutes of operation
Interior Emergency Lighting—Consists of:
- ♦ Door   ♦ Aisle   ♦ Cross-Aisle
- ♦ Escape Path   ♦ Exit Lights   ♦ Luminescent Exit Lights

Escape Path Lighting
  Installed in arm rests
  Designed to light path if smoke obscures lights above four feet from floor of cabin
Battery-powered exit lights at each cabin exit
Exterior Emergency Lighting
Lights aft of each door illuminate slide areas
Door 2L and 2R have lights built into the slide
  Slides have a sharper angle from the fuselage than slides at other doors
  Lighting designed to prevent "missing the slide"

Cockpit Lighting

Mag compass light is controlled with **GLARESHIELD** rheostat
Master brightness control—optimized when all controls with dots are adjusted to line up the dot and the marker line

Passenger Internet/Broadband Switch

Broadband Switch
OFF—disables two way broadband passenger communications.
ON—(guarded position) – enables two way broadband passenger communications.

Doors and Windows

Flight Deck Door

Reinforced doors installed throughout fleet
Door code located in secure file **RF 7700 CODE**
Additional information in OMV1

Flight Deck Windows

Provide emergency exit from cockpit with escape ropes
Can be closed in flight if unlocked on takeoff
  Recommended not to exceed V_{REF} + 80
  May not be possible to close above 250 knots

Passenger Entry Doors

8 Doors—All translating, plug-type doors and operate the same
  Numbered front to rear **1-4**, **L** or **R** (i.e. **1L**, **4R**, etc.)
Flight Lock
  Each door automatically locks when airspeed is >80 knots
  Spring-loaded solenoid held locked with electrical power
  Unlock occurs with loss of electrical power
Slide Deployment
  With doors armed, occurs when door opened from inside
  Disarmed when door is opened from outside
Vent Panels
  Connected to door handles
  Insure cabin is depressurized before door opens
  At <u>high</u> differential pressures, vent panel opens only partially until differential pressure is reduced
  At <u>very high</u> differential pressure, panel can't be opened
Indicators
  Power assist reservoir—if gas needle outside green zone, system is unusable
  Slide / Raft gas bottle pressure gauge—if gas needle outside green zone, system is unusable
  Girt Bar Indicator Flag viewing windows
    Yellow—Door and slide / raft *are* armed
    Black—Door and slide / raft *are not* armed

Cargo Doors

Forward and aft cargo doors— Open outward
  Latched closed, not plug-type doors
  Electrically operated
Bulk cargo door—Plug-type door
  Manually opened
  Opens inward Door Synoptic Display

Symbols used for Passenger Doors
Amber		....................................Door Open
Blank		...................................Door Closed
White		...................Door Status Not Available

Symbols used for Cargo Doors
Amber		....................................Door Open
Blank		...................................Door Closed
White		...................Door Status Not Available

Oxygen Systems

Flight Crew Oxygen System

One bottle supplies all cockpit masks (4)
Squeezing red mask release levers releases the mask from storage
Removing the mask:
  Inflates the mask harness
  Momentarily displays the yellow O2 flow indicator
  Selects the mask microphone in the removed mask (deselecting boom mic)
Reselecting boom mic
  Close left mask door *and*
  Press and release the **RESET/TEST** switch

Passenger Oxygen System

O₂ supplied from individual chemical O₂ generators
Located in passenger service units (PSUs) above passenger seats
Oxygen flows for a minimum of 12 minutes
300ER Oxygen flows for minimum of 22 minutes

Masks deployed:
Automatically—cabin altitude exceeds approx. 13,500'
pressure
300ER Horn sounds in cockpit and crew rest
area
Manually when cockpit overhead panel Passenger
Oxygen Switch pressed to the **ON** position

Switch Indications
Blank—Normal position, system ready
Pressed—Signals PSU switches to drop masks
ON (*Amber*)—System is operating and masks have
dropped

Emergency Equipment

Emergency Evacuation Signal System

Alerts Flight Attendants to evacuate passenger cabin
Switches located:
On the flight deck center console
At each flight attendant station

Operation
Flight Deck Evacuation Switch **ON** activates evacuation signal:
In cockpit **and**
On flight attendant panels
Flight Deck Evacuation Switch **ARM**
Pressing flight attendant panel **EVAC COMMAND** switch activates evacuation command signals:
On the flight attendant panels **and**
On the flight deck
Flight Deck Evacuation Switch **OFF**;
Pressing flight attendant panel **EVAC COMMAND** switch activates evacuation command signals:
On the flight deck **ONLY**

Halon Fire Extinguishers

Halon Gas is toxic and inhalation is very dangerous
Works by displacing oxygen
Halon is heavier than other gases and will fall to the lower areas (floor vicinity)
Warning: *If a fire extinguisher is discharged in the flight deck area, all flight crew members must wear O₂ masks and use 100% oxygen with emergency selected*

Emergency Locator Transmitters

Installed in slide/raft containers at doors 1L and 4R (**300ER** 5R)

Transmit automatically when slide / rafts are deployed in the water
300ER **ELT Switch**
RESET—(spring-loaded) ends ELT transmission
ARMED—(guarded) Transmits emergency signal if activated by high deceleration forces
ON—transmits emergency locator signal.

Emergency Flashlights

Located at each flight attendant seat
Come on automatically
When removed from the holders
Cannot be turned off until returned to holder
Charging lights
Small LED flashes continuously if batteries serviceable
If no flashing light—battery replacement is called for

Enhanced Medical Kits and Automatic External Defibrillators (AEDs)

Locked into position with a bracket
Can be unlocked with cockpit door key
Neither is required for dispatch

200ER Aircraft Principal Dimensions

Width	199' 11"	60.9m
Length	209' 1"	63.7m
Height	60' 5" to 61' 6"	18.4-18.8m
Main Gear Strut Width	36'	11m
Nose to Mains	84'11"	25.9m

For other dimensions, see
OM Volume II, AIRPLANE GENERAL-10.1-10.2
For turn radius and taxi details, see
OM Volume II, AIRPLANE GENERAL-10.1-10.2
or OM Volume I TAXI-TAKEOFF 10.6-10.7

Boeing 777 200ER Dimensions
Boeing 777 300ER Dimensions
Both Versions

209'1" (63.7m)
239'9" 73.08m

84'11" (25.88m)
102'5" (31.22m)

49'11" (15.2 m)
70'8" (21.53m)

36' (10.97 m)

199'11" (60.9m)
212'7" 64.8m

Steering Angle 70°

Nose Radius
110' (33.5m)
131.2' (40.0 m)

Tail Radius
95' (29.0 m)
147.1' (44.8 m)

Wing Tip Radius
145' (44.2m)
160.2' (48.8m)

Center of turn for minimum turning radius. (Slow continuous turning with minimum thrust on all engines. No differential braking.)

Minimum Pavement Width for 180° Turn
156' (47.5m)
185.5'(56.5m)

Side Silhouette drawing courtesy of **Norebbo Stock Illustration and Design**, *www.norebbo.com.*

Emergency Equipment Location

200ER

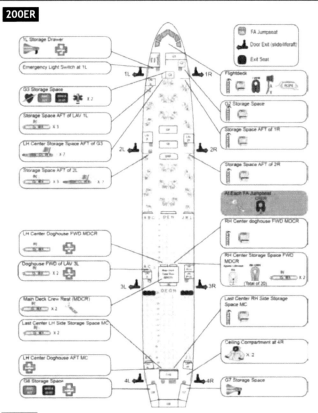

300ER

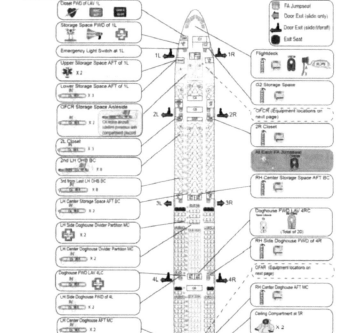

300ER Overhead Flight Crew Rest Area

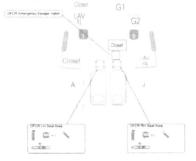

300ER Overhead FA Rest Area

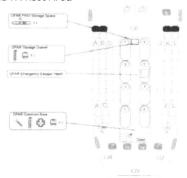

All Diagrams:
OMV1, Systems > Aircraft General > Emergency Equipment

Aircraft Configuration

	Code	First	Business	Coach	Total	Ship Numbers
-200ER	AF		45	215	260	Various
	83		35	247	282	Various
-300ER	82	8	52	250	310	All

Air Conditioning and Pressurization

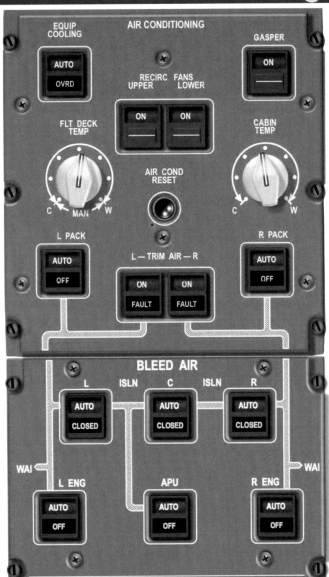

Bleed Air System

Engine Bleed Air

Valves are pressure actuated
Remain closed until sufficient pressure exists to cause forward flow
Engine bleed valves **close automatically:**
◆ During engine start
◆ Bleed source loss
◆ Bleed air overtemperature
◆ Bleed air overpressure
◆ Bleed air duct leak
◆ Engine fire switch pulled
◆ Ground air cart supplying air

APU Bleed Air Supply

Primary Uses
◆ Engine start   ◆ Ground air conditioning
◆ Pressurization for no engine bleed takeoffs
300ER APU to Pack selection for takeoff accomplished through FMC

In flight use
Bleed air available up to 22,000 feet pressure altitude
Check valve in APU supply line prevents reverse flow back into APU

Ground Bleed Air Supply

Three connection points to bleed ducts
Check valves in supply line prevents reverse flow back into external sources

Duct Leak and Overheat Detection

If duct leak is detected, system automatically isolates the leak
Isolation process
May take one, two or three automatic steps
During process, bleed valves cycle and appropriate EICAS messages illuminate
When affected temperature cools
EICAS messages removed
System remains isolated
Switch **OFF** or **CLOSED** lights remain and show final status

Air Synoptic

Selected temperatures are magenta
Not displayed when temperature control of associated zone is inoperative
Actual temperatures are white

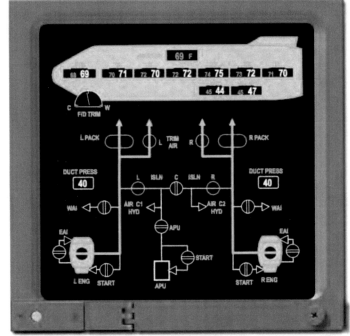

Air Conditioning System

Packs

Two identical controllers on each pack
If a controller fails, the other is automatically selected
Pack output is increased during high demands **OR**
To compensate for a failed pack or recirc fan
Pack output is reduced flow during high bleed air demand periods such as gear retraction **AND**
During cruise flight to reduce fuel consumption
Ground operation
Dual pack operation is the normal mode
Fuel flow approximately the same with 1 or 2 packs operating
Noise level is higher with single pack operation
Non-Normal Operation
Protections are automatic for
Pack control
Fault detection
Overheat protection
If a significant fault is detected
Pack shuts down automatically
EICAS Message **PACK L** or **R** displays
Attempt to restore pack operation may be made by pressing
Air Conditioning Reset switch

Pack Switches
AUTO—pack control is automatic
OFF (**AUTO** not visible)—off
OFF—pack flow control valve commanded closed
Illuminated when:
♦ the PACK switch is pushed **OFF** OR
♦ Pack valve is failed closed, OR
♦ Pack or compressor outlet high temperature OR
♦ Bleed air pressure is inadequate, OR
♦ **300ER** R PACK valve is closed during APU to Pack Takeoff procedure

Standby Cooling Mode

Backup to normal mode
EICAS Message **PACK MODE L** or **R** displays
STBY COOLING (Amber) Displays on Air Synoptic
Packs may be in different modes
If one pack standby and other normal
Pack in standby shuts down at "lower altitudes and higher ambient temperatures"
Occurs if ambient conditions do not allow standby cooling to be effective
Pack restarts in standby when conditions suitable for standby operation
If operating in standby mode on ground
Pack is selected off until airborne
When ambient air conditions allow for sufficient cooling, pack is selected on in standby mode
Pack is shut down when descent to lower altitudes occurs
If both packs standby cooling mode OR one pack INOP and the other in standby cooling mode,
Pack(s) operate continuously to maintain cabin pressurization
No shutdown occurs at lower altitudes
A single pack in standby cooling mode is sufficient to maintain pressure at cruise altitudes
In standby cooling mode
Pack cooling capacity is reduced
Warmer temperatures in cabin and flight deck may result
Note: Description of what happens in standby mode removed from OM; Previous OM editions described standby mode as heat exchanger only cooling

Air Distribution

Flight deck air source
100% Comes from left pack only
Flight deck pressure slightly higher than cabin
Prevents cabin smoke from entering flight deck
Air Flow from Cabin and Flight Deck
Air flows to lower deck
Then either exhausted through outflow valves or
Drawn into lower recirculation system
Air from lower recirculation fans
Mixes with pack air
Then enters lower deck distribution ducts
Air from upper recirculation fans
Flows into lower deck distribution ducts
Recirculation Fans
Either fan off causes packs to operate at full flow
Cabin exchange rate is increased
Fuel consumption increases 0.7% for each fan switch turned **OFF**
Recirculation fan switches—see next page

Temperature Control

Trim Air System
Mixes hot trim air with cooled pack air to moderate flow to various zones
Pack outflow determined by zone requesting coolest air
Trim Air Switches
ON—Trim air valve is commanded open.
Off (ON not visible)—Trim air valve is commanded closed, AND
FAULT illuminates.
FAULT
The trim air valve is failed closed OR
The trim air valve is commanded closed because of a zone supply duct overheat OR
Trim Air Switch is selected **OFF**.

Cabin Temperature Selector
Sets master reference temperature between 65 and 85°F
Flight attendants can vary individual zone temperatures by ±10°F from master temperature
Flight Deck Temperature Control
Sets flight deck temperature in range 65-85°F (75°±10°)
If neither controller is available to pack temperature controller
Pack outlet temperature is regulated to achieve either:
The last temperature set or
An average cabin temperature of 75°F
Complete loss of temperature controllers
Can occur with:
Failure of both controllers or
Loss of electrical power
Air supply and cabin pressurization controllers control pack flow control valves
Pack flow rate is modulated to achieve pack outlet temperature in 40-110°F range
All flight deck temperature control disabled except pack control switches

Cargo Temperature Control

Forward Cargo Area
Heated by warm air from forward equipment ventilation system
No selectable temperature control available
Aft and bulk cargo areas—
Switches available for temperature regulation
OFF—shuts off bleed air to compartment
With temperature selector set to **LOW** and TAT less than 7°C (45°F)
Respective temperature control valve opens
Compartment temperature is maintained between 40 and 50°F.
With temperature selector set to **HIGH** and TAT less than 21°C (70°F)
Respective temperature control valve opens
Compartment temperature is maintained between 65 and 75°F
Overheat Protection
Automatically shuts down bulk cargo heating if overheat is detected
If triggered, cargo heat to the related compartment cannot be restored in flight
Insulated curtain separates the two compartments

Equipment Cooling

Forward Equipment cooling
Supplies cooling air to electrical and electronic equipment
On the flight deck
In the forward E&E compartment racks
System uses internal fans and valves to
Draw cooling air from cabin and force it through equipment racks and flight deck equipment
Vents warmed air to two places
Directly out outflow valve OR
Directs some of the air into forward cargo* compartment if it requires additional heat
If system is inoperative on the ground
Ground crew call horn sounds
EICAS advisory message **EQUIP COOLING**
Override Mode
In flight—forward system is **automatically** reconfigured when **any** of the following occur (**SEFFF**—**S**moke, **E**quipment, **F**low, **F**ans, **F**ire):
♦ **Smoke** is detected in the forward equipment cooling system or forward equipment ventilation system
♦ **Equipment** cooling switch is **OFF**
♦ Low **Flow** is detected in flight
♦ Both supply **Fans** fail in the forward equipment ventilation system in flight
♦ Forward cargo **Fire** extinguishing system is **ARMED**

Manually commanded by the equipment cooling switch when placed in **OVRD**
  In flight, use of this switch "aids smoke evacuation from flight deck"
System changes in override mode
  Both supply fans off
  Vent valve opens
  Cabin differential pressure is used to reverse airflow and exhaust air (and smoke, if present)
  Air exits through override valve to an overboard vent

AUTO—system operating normally
  AUTO off (not in view)—any of the following exist:
  ♦ Both equipment cooling supply fans are **_not_** operating
  ♦ Override valve is open
  ♦ Forward cargo heat valve is closed
  ♦ Airflow in Override mode
  ♦ **300ER** Nitrogen generation system (NGS) is shut down
  OVRD—on when ECS configures to override mode:
  ♦ Both equipment cooling supply fans are failed, **OR**
  ♦ Smoke is detected in the equipment cooling system **OR**
  ♦ **EQUIP COOLING** switch is off **OR**
  ♦ **CARGO FIRE ARM FWD** switch is in **ARMED**
  Flow is "adequate" in cruise
  Decreases as airplane descends due to lower differential cabin pressure

Aft Equipment Cooling
System provides
  Cooling and ventilating air to aft electronic equipment
  Ventilating air for lavatories and galleys
Two fans—primary and backup
Conditioned air is supplied to galleys from air distribution system
Aft equipment cooling system fans draw air from
  ♦ Aft electronic equipment ♦ Galleys ♦ Lavatories
Air discharges through aft outflow valve

Recirc Fan Switches
Two switches—
  Upper Switch controls forward and aft upper Recirc fans
  Lower Switch controls left and right lower Recirc fans
When one or both recirculation fan switches are **OFF**
  Packs operate at full flow
  Cabin air exchange rate is increased
  Fuel consumption increases 0.7% for each fan switch **OFF**.

Pressurization

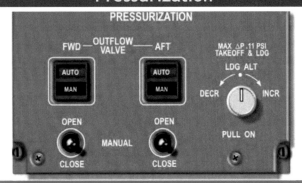

Outflow and Control Valves
Two outflow valves
  Forward and aft
  Most airflow is out aft valve—improves ventilation and smoke removal
  Either valve can control pressure if other fails
Two positive pressure relief valves
Four negative pressure relief doors

Automatic operation
Selected when outflow valve switches are set to **AUTO**
Inputs from
  ♦ Ambient pressure on ground
  ♦ Flight plan data from flight management computer
  Uses these to calculate pressurization schedule

Pressurization Schedule
  Small positive pressure on ground
  Increases to maximum cabin differential pressure
  Climb of cabin then becomes variable with airplane climb
  At maximum certified cruise altitude, cabin pressure is 8,000 feet pressure altitude
  On descent, pressure is gradually increased to slightly below landing field pressure altitude
  On touchdown, both outflow valves open to depressurize cabin
Landing Altitude
  Departure field altitude is retained in memory in case of return to point of origin
  Arrival field is planned descent point after:
  ♦ 400 NM from departure airport **OR**
  ♦ Half way to destination
  Whichever occurs first
LANDING ALT EICAS Message—Indicates
  ♦ Landing altitude is unavailable from the FMC
  ♦ No landing altitude set in MAN
  Cabin altitude controller assumes a landing altitude of 2000 feet MSL

Manual Operation
Selected when outflow valves are set to **MAN**
Outflow valves then manually operated by moving related valve switch to open or close
Valve position displays on EICAS when in manual mode
  Moving from full open to full closed takes 30 seconds
Landing altitude selection
  Can be accomplished with landing altitude selector
  Pulling switch out
    Removes FMC landing altitude
    Displays pressurization indications on EICAS

Operation with Loss of Cabin Pressure
If Sudden loss of pressure occurs
  Outflow valves close to control pressure loss
  When inside and outside pressures equalize, outflow valves open
  Protects airplane from negative overpressure
Crew should not manually close valves in this case

Pressurization System Indications
Appears on EICAS for abnormal pressurization events
Displays when (associate with items on display)

	18	DUCT PRESS	18	FWD	AFT
CAB ALT	7500	RATE	+250	OP	
LDG ALT	200	AUTO ΔP	5.6	CL	

  ♦ Duct pressure is below normal range (*Amber*) with respective engine running
  ♦ Cabin altitude is above normal range (*off schedule*)
  ♦ EICAS **CABIN ALTITUDE** message is displayed (*Red*: >10,000')
  ♦ Landing altitude selector is pulled **ON**
  ♦ Cabin differential pressure above normal (*Amber*)
  ♦ Cabin differential pressure is excessive (*Red*)
  ♦ Air synoptic is on any MFD
  ♦ An outflow valve switch is selected to **MAN**
  ♦ Abnormal air-related EICAS messages have occurred:
    CABIN ALTITUDE AUTO
    LANDING ALTITUDE
    OUTFLOW VALVE FWD
    OUTFLOW VALVE AFT

Key Cabin Pressure Altitudes
  >8500' Cabin pressure—Display turns amber
  >10,000' Cabin pressure—Display turns red
  >13,500' Cabin pressure—PSU Masks drop automatically

Miscellaneous
Shoulder and foot heaters
Provided for Captain and First Officer seats

Acronyms
ASCPC ....Air supply cabin pressure controller
PRSOV ....Pressure regulating and shut off valve

Anti-Ice and Rain Protection

Automatic Ice Detection System

General Features
Detects icing in flight
Inhibited on the ground
Signals sent to both engine and wing anti-ice **when:** In flight **and**
Systems are in **AUTO**
Two probes
One on each **side of forward fuselage**
Automatically deiced **if ice-buildup is sensed**

Operation
When either probe detects ice buildup <u>more than once</u>
Engine anti-ice valves automatically open
Engine cowls are de-iced
When either probe detects ice buildup <u>several times</u>
Wing anti-ice valves automatically open
Six wing leading edge slats (three per wing) de-iced
In both cases, valves close when system no longer detects icing

Engine & Wing Anti-Ice Systems

Engine Anti-Ice System
Bleed air heats engine
cowls only when
ice is detected
May be operated in
flight or on the
ground
In flight, **AUTO**
normally used
On ground, manual
(**ON**) must be used

Each engine has its own independent system
Leak detection
Dual loop anti-ice duct leak detection system on each engine
If duct leak is detected, affected
engine anti-ice valve closes
Engine anti ice annunciation is on N_1
gauge of EICAS
EAI Indication shows engine anti-
ice ON

Wing Anti-Ice System (WAI)
Can be operated in flight only
Inhibited on ground, regardless of switch position
Automatic Wing Anti-Ice Inhibits—when ALL of the following:
♦ TAKEOFF Mode is selected **AND**
♦ Less than 10 minutes has elapsed from liftoff
Wing Anti Ice Inhibits
♦ If TAT > 10°C, WAI is inhibited for 5 minutes after liftoff
♦ **TAKEOFF** mode is selected, **and** less than 10 minutes has
elapsed after liftoff
Mid-Wing Leading Edge Slats deiced by
WAI system
3 LE Slats (out of 7) on each
wing
Slats are numbered from
left
wingtip across to
right
wing tip
Leading edge slats
3, 4, 5, 10, 11, & 12 are deiced (*Slat numbering from previous OM*)
Symmetry Protection
If a bleed source is lost **and** duct isolation has **not** occurred:
Isolation valves open automatically to maintain anti-icing
to both wings
If one wing anti-ice valve fails closed:
Other is automatically closed to prevent asymmetric wing
anti-icing

Leak Detection Systems
System senses and isolates duct leaks automatically
See *AIR section* for details
Wing Anti-Ice Annunciation (WAI)
Displayed below EICAS N_1
indications when a wing anti-ice
valve is open

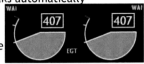

Window Heat

Forward Windows
Exterior surface anti-icing
Interior surface anti-fogging
Backup antifogging system operates automatically in the event
of a primary system failure

Side Windows
Interior surface anti-fogging only

Window Heat Switches (4)
Control heating for all flight deck windows
With switches ON, window heat operates as soon as power is
available
Thermal shock prevented by gradual increase in heating when
power is applied
Switch positions
Pressed—ON;
Window heat is
applied to
selected windows
This is normal
position
Released—Off, **INOP** indication illuminated
INOP—(*Amber*) Switch is off **OR**
Overheat is detected **OR**
System fault has occurred
Backup Window Heat Switches
Overhead Maintenance Panel
Allows removal of power in the event of
window damage
Controls arcing and smoke danger
Documented—QRH **Window Damage L, R**
procedure ....See QRH AIRPLANE GENERAL 1.21

Windshield Wipers
L and R Switches
Self Explanatory

Probe Heat
Components heated when either engine is
running
3 Pitot Probes
2 Angle of Attack vanes
Component heated only in flight—TAT probe

Acronyms
WAI ....Wing anti-Ice
EAI ....Engine anti-ice
PRSOV..........................Pressure regulating and shut off valve

Autoflight

Editor's Note: *This section covers systems-related notes which are considered helpful for understanding the relationship between the autopilot and other aircraft systems. No attempt is made to summarize the operation of the autoflight system, as it is better learned in the CPT and through Plato than through this medium. In addition, normal interaction with the system keeps pilots aware of the capabilities, techniques and options which work well in flight. For that reason, notes here are intended for systems review more than for initial instruction.*

Overview

Components of Automatic Flight Control System
Autopilot Flight Director System (AFDS)
Autothrottle System

Control
Mode Control Panel (MCP)
   Select mode engagement
   Insert clearance specifics such as heading and altitude
   Override computer planned parameters
   Selected altitude (*as well as actual aircraft altitude*) is transmitted to ATC
Flight Management Computer (FMC)
   Upload and activate route for flight plan
   Set planned parameters, such as
      Crossing altitudes
      Cruise speed and altitude
      Performance and weight and balance parameters
      Takeoff data

Autopilot

Autopilot Flight Director System
Components
   3 Autopilot flight director computers (AFDCs),
      Control flight directors & autopilots
      Does not control flight control surfaces directly
      Sends inputs to the autopilots,
      Autopilots send commands to flight control surfaces through fly-by-wire flight control system
      Rudder control
         Not normally accomplished through autopilot *except*, during
            Autopilot approach and landing
            Nosewheel steering and rudder during rollout
         For more information on rudder control, see Flight Control chapter, *page 39* of this study guide
   Mode Control Panel (MCP) which controls
      Autopilot
      Flight director
      Altitude alert
      Autothrottles
      Select and activate AFDS modes
      Setting of
         Altitudes
         Speeds
         Climb and descent profiles
Mode Selection
   Press mode button
      Green bar in bottom half of mode switch illuminates
      Confirms mode armed or engaged
   Pressing any other button deselects original mode and selects new one

FLCH

Exception:
   APP mode will not deselect after capturing localizer and glide slope
To disengage **APP**:
   Disconnect autopilot *and* turn off both flight directors
   OR Engage go-around mode
   OR if above 1500' radio altitude, press APP mode switch again
      Default roll and pitch modes result
Some mode switches can be disengaged by pressing a second time:
   ♦ VNAV   ♦ LNAV
   ♦ LOC   ♦ APP (*See notes above*)

Autopilot
Engagement—Press either of two MCP autopilot engage switches
   Disengagement
   Four ways to disengage
      ♦Press either control wheel autopilot disengage switch
      ♦MCP autopilot disengage bar
      ♦Override with control column or control wheel
      ♦With LAND2 or LAND3 annunciated, can override with rudder pedals as well
Results
   EICAS warning, **AUTOPILOT DISC**
   Warning results whether manual or automatic disconnect occurs
Degradation
   Autopilot detects mode degradation
   Remains in attitude stabilizing mode based on inertial data
   Persistent degradation results in
      Amber line through modes on affected flight mode on PFD
      EICAS Caution **AUTOPILOT** message
   If degradation clears, mode annunciation displays inside green box

Autopilot engagement is recommended with less than 4000 RVR (1200 m) or 3/4 mile visibility

Uncommanded Turns in LNAV
Have been reported
When observed, FMC CDU prematurely sequenced a point
   May occur when within *1 NM* of active waypoint for small route modifications, *OR*
   Within *4 NM* of active waypoint for modifications involving a large turn
Prevention—Avoid:
   ♦ Executing lateral OFFSET when approaching an active waypoint
   ♦ Entry of a vertical or lateral flight planning change when approaching an active waypoint.
   ♦ Executing DIR-TO with ABEAM selected when approaching an active waypoint.

Flight Director

Flight Director Display

Steering bars in view when
Respective (L/R) FD switch is on
If switch off, pressing a TO/GA switch displays FD bars

Degradation
If degradation sensed, FD provides attitude stabilizing commands based on inertial data
Persistent degradation results in removal of steering bars from PFD
Mode self clears if fault disappears

Stall or Overspeed Protection also result in FD bars disappearing from PFDs

AFDS Modes

Status Annunciation—appears on PFD above attitude indication
FLT DIR—FD is on and A/P *is not* engaged
A/P—FD is on and A/P *is* engaged
LAND3—3 A/Ps are operating normally for autoland
A single fault cannot prevent the autopilot system from making an automatic landing
Status is considered <u>fail operational</u>
LAND2—AFDS redundancy is reduced
In some cases, only 2 A/Ps are available
A single fault cannot cause the autopilot system to make significant deviation from flight path
Status is considered <u>fail passive</u>
NO AUTOLAND—AFDS is unable to make autolanding
Changes in status
Result in aural alert
Alert inhibited until after touchdown when not affecting safety of flight
Below 200 feet RA, all except **NO AUTOLAND** are inhibited

Mode Annunciation—appears just above PFD AFDS status annunciation
Three sections, left to right, are

Autothrottle	Roll	Pitch
SPD	LNAV	VNAV
	LOC	G/S

Mode Indications
Green large letters at top—Engaged
White smaller letters at bottom of block—armed

Autothrottle modes
THR—Thrust applied to maintain V/S required by engaged pitch mode
THR REF—Thrust set to limit displayed on EICAS
IDLE—Displayed while autothrottle moves to idle
When at idle, mode changes to **HOLD**
HOLD—Autothrottle servos disabled
SPD—Autothrottles adjust to maintain set speed
Note: *A/T selection inhibited on takeoff from 50 KIAS to 400'AGL*

Roll Modes
LNAV <u>Armed</u>—Will engage when parameters met
<u>Engaged</u>—LNAV is tracking active route displayed on the ND if aircraft is:
Above 50 feet AGL (radio altitude) and
Within 2½ NM of active route leg
HDG
HDG SEL—Airplane is turning to or tracking heading set in MCP heading/track window
HDG HOLD—If wings level when **HOLD** selected, AFDS holds that preset heading
If in a turn when **HOLD** selected, holds heading at rollout
TRK, TRK SEL, TRK HOLD—Same as **HDG** above, except maintaining the track, not the heading
LOC
<u>Armed</u>—AFDS captures the localizer when
Within range *and*
Within 120° of localizer track
<u>Engaged</u>—AFDS maintains localizer course
TO/GA
<u>Ground</u>—Mode is engaged by selecting either FD **ON** when both FDs are **OFF**
Mode guidance becomes active at liftoff

<u>Flight</u>—Armed with flaps not retracted OR at glideslope capture
No annunciation for armed in flight
Engaged by pressing a **TO/GA** switch
AFDS maintains ground track present at mode engagement

ROLLOUT
<u>Armed</u>—Displayed below 1500' RA
<u>Engaged</u>—Engagement occurs at 2' RA
Rudder and NW steering used to maintain aircraft on centerline

Pitch Modes
TO/GA
Ground—Engaged when
Either FD is turned on when both had been off **OR**
By pressing either **TO/GA** switch with airspeed over 80 knots
Roll guidance active at lift-off
Note: *Pressing* **TO/GA** *> 80 knots IAS disarms* **LNAV** *and* **VNAV**
After takeoff, AFDS commands pitch to maintain
V_2 (based on speed set before takeoff) plus 15 knots **OR**
If airspeed remains above target for 5 seconds, target reset to current speed **OR**
IAS/Mach window speed if the value is changed to a speed greater than the target speed
In flight other than takeoff, armed when flaps not retracted (no annunciation in flight)
After go-around initiated
Commanded speed is the higher of
MCP IAS / MACH window **OR**
Current speed *to a maximum of* MCP IAS / MACH window speed plus 25
GA is displayed as thrust limit on primary EICAS engine display
Note: **300ER** *During go-around from* **LAND 2** *or* **LAND 3** *approach, automatic* **LNAV** *activation causes disengagement of autopilot rudder control. If executing an engine out missed approach with thrust asymmetry compensation inoperative, manual rudder control may be required to prevent large roll and yaw excursions.*

VNAV—<u>Armed</u> by pressing **VNAV** switch
<u>Engages</u> above 400' on takeoff if armed
Note: *400' is referenced to baro altitude recorded at 100 knots on takeoff roll.*
VNAV SPD—Maintains FMC speed displayed on PFD and/or CDU **CLIMB** or **DESCENT** pages
If speed intervention used, MCP **IAS/MACH** selector is used to set speed
VNAV PTH—AFDS maintains FMC altitude or descent path with pitch commands
As aircraft approaches top of descent with cruise altitude still set, CDU scratchpad message **RESET MCP ALT** displays
VNAV ALT—Altitude is maintained or captured
If conflict occurs between VNAV profile and MCP altitude
Airplane levels at MCP altitude *and*
Flight mode annunciation becomes **VNAV ALT**

V/S Pressing mode switch
Opens vertical speed window to display current vertical speed
Allows changing commanded vertical speed with **V/S** wheel
Pitch maintains rate of climb or descent selected in **VS/FPA** window

FPA—Selected by pressing **VS/FPA** mode button *and*
Pressing small black **VS/FPA** selector button on MCP
AFDS maintains pitch as required to track commanded flight path angle

FLCH SPD—Selected by pressing mode button
IAS/MACH window opens and displays current IAS
AFDS adjust pitch as needed to maintain selected IAS/MACH window airspeed or mach

ALT—Altitude hold mode is engaged
Engaged by pressing MCP altitude hold switch, **OR**
Capturing the selected altitude from a **V/S**, **FPA** or **FLCH** climb or descent

G/S—AFDS is tracking ILS glideslope
  Can capture when within 80° of localizer course
  Capture may occur before localizer capture
FLARE
  Armed—on autoland, displayed below 1500' RA
  Engaged—between 60 and 40 feet RA
    Accomplishes autoland flare maneuver so the AFDS can
      transition to **ROLLOUT** mode

Autothrottle System

Autothrottle operation

Thrust control from takeoff through landing
Can be used without FD or Autopilot
  Available modes include
    THR REF   SPD   HOLD   IDLE
Use during manual landing
  Thrust reduces to idle at 25' RA
  This occurs in any mode *except* **TO/GA** or **FLCH**
Can be overridden at any time by pressing either A/T disconnect
  switch on thrust levers

Autothrottle Automatic Arming—occurs automatically if:
  <u>All of the following conditions are met:</u>
    ♦ Autothrottle is functional (no system faults)
    ♦ Airplane altitude above 100' RA on approach or airplane
       barometric altitude 400 feet above airport on
       takeoff
    ♦ No autopilot or flight director is active OR
       An A/P or FD is in **VNAV**, **FPA**, **ALT**, **V/S**, or **GS**
  <u>And both of the following occur:</u>
    ♦ Speed less than FMC calculated for one second
    ♦ Thrust below reference thrust

Automatic Disarming—occurs automatically if:
  Fault in active A/T mode detected
  Override—Thrust Levers overridden manually after A/T has
    begun to retard to idle
  Reverse lever—either one raised to reverse idle
  Shut Off—engines both shut down

Autothrottle "Wake Up" Mode
  Allows stall protection when armed but not activated
  Activates when speed decreases to near stick shaker
    activation
  Advances in **SPD** or **THR REF** modes to maintain the greater of
    ♦ Minimum maneuvering speed (top of amber band) *<u>or</u>*
    ♦ Speed set in the mode control speed window
  Does *<u>not</u>* activate in the following conditions
    ♦ Pitch modes **FLCH** or **TOGA** *<u>OR</u>*
    ♦ Airplane below 400' AGL (takeoff) or below 100' AGL on
      approach
    Note: *During descent in* **VNAV SPD**, *autothrottle may*
      activate in **HOLD** *mode and will not support stall*
      protection

Abnormal Operation

EICAS Messages for servo failure
  AUTOTHROTTLE L or **R** —respective servo failure
PFD Status message for one A/T only armed
  L or **R** precedes status, indicating only that A/T is engaged in
    the specified mode
  Example: **L SPD**

Autothrottle Uncommanded Motion

Has been reported during cruise flight
Prevention
  Prior to engine start, move the FMC selector switch to either L
    or R, then back to AUTO
  Cycling of the switch inflight at any time will resolve or
    prevent the anomaly

Automation Key Altitudes & Speeds

Takeoff

Below 50 Knots—Pressing **TO/GA** switch engages thrust reference
  (**THR REF**) mode
50 knots or above—If A/T not engaged, cannot be engaged until
  above 400'
80 Knots—Mode changes to **HOLD**
Over 80 Knots—Pressing a **TO/GA** switch disarms **LNAV** and **VNAV**
100 knots—FMC records barometric altitude; used for:
  Engaging **VNAV** if armed when 400' above this altitude
  Enabling autothrottle activation if not active
  Commanding acceleration altitude for flap retraction
  Set climb thrust if altitude entered on MCP Takeoff page 2
If engine failure occurs on the ground, pitch command target
  speed at liftoff is the greater of V_2 **OR**
    Airspeed at liftoff

Climb

Lift Off—Pitch commanded to maintain:
  Target speed of V_2+15
  If speed is above target speed for 5 seconds, target is reset
    to current airspeed limited to V_2+25
If engine failure occurs after lift-off, pitch command target
  speed is:
  If airspeed is below V_2...
    V_2
  If airspeed between V_2 and V_2+15 ....Existing
    speed
  If airspeed above V_2+15 ....
    V_2+15
After Liftoff—if **TO/GA** pressed with A/T engaged:
  Thrust Lever derates are removed
  A/T engages in **THR REF**
50' RA—LNAV engages if armed
400 feet above active runway elevation
  VNAV engages if armed
  A/T sets selected reference thrust and annunciates **THR REF**
Acceleration height—pitch commands speed to takeoff flap
  placard speed minus 5 knots
Flap retraction completion—VNAV commanded speed is greater
  of:
  250 Knots or
  V_{REF} + 80 Knots
Thrust reduction point
  Altitude in MCP takeoff page 2 **OR**
  Flap retraction
  FMC changes thrust limit to armed climb limit—**CLB**, **CLB1**, or
    CLB2

Communications

Cockpit Voice Recorder System

Records inputs from:
Flight deck through area mic
Communications channels from any audio control panel
300ER Status
Indicator in place of meter—illuminates after successful test
Extinguishes after test button is released
Records continuously
300ER Also records datalink communications
300ER Records for 10 minutes after AC power is off
Cockpit Voice Recorder Circuit Breaker
Location—E&E P110 panel (F6—labeled **VOX RCDR**)
Procedures requiring pulling breaker..QRH GENERAL 2.12-2.13

VHF Communications

Three receiver/transmitters
Left—Configured for voice only
Center—Normally configured for data for ACARS
Right—Normally voice, may be configured for data,
To change from DATA to voice
Select a voice frequency
Transfer frequency to active side of window
200 **Hot Mic Protection**
Ground with both engines shut down
A VHF which transmits more than 35 seconds
Automatically disabled
Dashes in the tuning panel window for that radio
Radio is reactivated when transmit button for that radio is released
Any other time—if VHF or HF radio transmits over 30 seconds
EICAS message—**RADIO TRANSMIT**
Message disappears after transmission ceases
300ER Hot Mic Protection—If a VHF radio transmits > 35 seconds:
♦ That radio is automatically disabled AND
♦ Dashes appear in the tuning panel frequency window AND
♦ Intermittent tone is heard through respective radio audio

HF Radios

Two radios, L and R
One antenna
May be used for reception on both simultaneously
Only one HF may transmit at a time—other deactivated during transmission
Tuning
First time transmitter is keyed after new frequency entered, frequency is tuned
Tone is heard while tuning takes place
Maximum tuning time is 7 seconds
A tone lasting over 7 seconds indicates a failure to tune
Last 100 frequencies are stored and tune quickly
If a frequency not in last 100 is tuned
Longer tone as frequency is tuned
Frequency is added to most recent 100 list

Communications Crew Alerting System

Provides visual and aural alerts to call crew's attention to various issues
Visual alerts—EICAS message with bullet symbol, i.e., **[?] COMM**
Aural Alert—High-low chime
Three Levels of Alert
High—not implemented currently
Medium—Visual and aural alert
Crew awareness required
Crew action may be required
Low—Visual alert only

SELCAL System (Selective Call)

Monitors 3 VHF and 2 HF radios
Alerts crew through communications crew alerting system

ACARS

All functions accomplished through ACARS Manager
When appropriate, use buttons on MFD screens **or**
Interactive buttons on glare shield
See COMMUNICATIONS 10.14, and 50.1 – 60.3

SATCOM (Satellite Communications)

Allows both voice and data communications
Three channels
Two dedicated for voice transmissions
One dedicated for data (ACARS)
EICAS Message [?] SATCOM MESSAGE
Indicates a SATCOM message requiring their attention on one of the CDU SATCOM pages
Servicing message clears EICAS message
Worldwide SATCOM System
Airplane Earth Station (AES) Segment
Airplane component
Includes antenna continuously aimed at satellite
Ground Earth Station (GES) segment
Ground component
Initiates and receives through ground antenna aimed at satellite
Satellite Segment—relays signals between AES and GES

Interphone Communication System

Flight Interphone System
Allows communication:
Between flight deck occupants
Between flight deck and ground crew
Selected with **INT** position of audio control panel
CALL
illumination in **INT** button
....indicates ground crew call
• **GROUND CALL** EICAS also indicates ground call
Service Interphone System
Voice communications allowed between ground crew stations at various locations around airplane
Connected to flight interphone system with Service Interphone Switch on overhead panel

SERV INTPH
OFF
ON

Cabin Interphone

Some of the following notes are from an unofficial handout, but the data has been confirmed to work
Normal Calls—
♦ Single hi-lo chime   ♦ EICAS msg: **CABIN CALL**

Door 1L/1R	11	Single Door, L	7<Door #>
Door 2L/2R	22	i.e. Door 1R	71
Door 3L/3R	33	Single Door, R	8<Door #>
Door 4L/4R	44	i.e. Door 4R	84

Priority Calls
♦ Single hi-lo chime   ♦ EICAS msg: **[?] CABIN ALERT**
Conference Calls
Multiple Calls, or clearing Calls when out of sync with incoming calls:
To delete multiple calls in queue use Center CDU
Press **DELETE**, then line select 1R or line showing the call to be deleted
*See further detail at **page 58** of this study guide,*
including operational notes and an interphone directory

Electrical Systems

System Overview

Main Electrical Sub-Systems

Main AC power—Primary source of all airplane electrical power
Backup Power
DC Power
Standby Power
Flight Control Power

Automated Features

System operation is automatic
Faults are automatically detected and isolated

AC Electrical System

Electrical Load Management System (ELMS)

Provides load management and protection
Ensures power is available to critical and essential equipment
Load Shedding
If loads exceed power available, sheds AC loads
Uses priorities to download until loads are within capacity available (airplane and/or external)
Order of shedding:
♦ Galleys
♦ Utility busses
♦ Individual equipment items powered by main AC busses
When additional power available or loads decrease, shed loads restored to power in reverse order
Synoptic Message—**LOAD SHED** Displays when conditions exist

AC Electrical System Power Sources

Aircraft Sources
L & R Engine integrated drive generators (IDG)
APU Generator
External—Primary and secondary external power
Requirements—Entire AC load can be supplied by any two main AC sources
Parallel versus Independent Power
Power sources are normally isolated from each other
During power source transfers on the ground
Operating sources momentarily paralleled
Prevents power interruption

Integrated Drive Generators (IDGs)

One on each engine—Automatic control and system protection functions
Connection to AC Busses—On engine start:
IDG automatically powers respective main bus
Previous power source is disconnected
Disconnection from AC Busses—An operating IDG may be disconnected from its bus by:
Pressing the generator control switch to **OFF**
Selecting an available external power source prior to engine shutdown
Generator Control Switch
ON—Arms generator breaker to automatically close when generator power is available
OFF—Opens field and generator breakers
Resets trip fault circuitry
Generator Drive Light

> **DRIVE**—
> *Without* generator **OFF** light
> Indicates <u>low oil pressure</u> on respective IDG
> EICAS message **ELEC GEN DRIVE L** *or* **R** displays
> *With* generator **OFF** light
> Indicates <u>high oil temperature</u> on respective IDG
> Disconnection is automatic in this case
> *Pressed*—Disconnects IDG Drive from Engine
> IDG Cannot be reconnected by flight crew

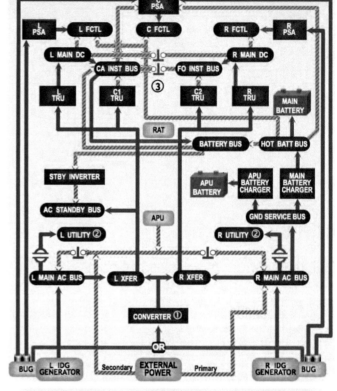

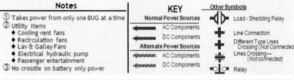

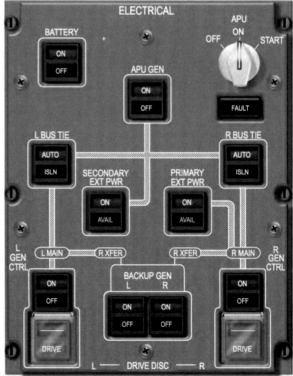

Electrical Synoptic
Comes up when ELEC synoptic display button is pressed

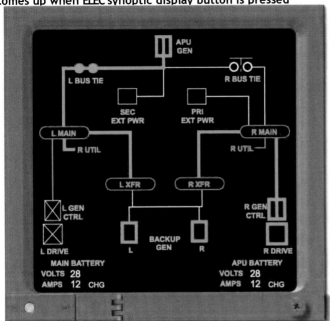

Electrical Synoptic Key

Power flowing (Green)	——	Drive disconnected (engine running) Amber	⊠
Power not flowing (White)	——	Not supplying power or failed (Amber)	⊠
Battery charging (White)	CHG	On or available (Green)	☐
Control (White)	CTRL		
Battery discharging (White)	DISCH	Off (White)	☐
Oil pressure low (Amber)	DRIVE		

APU Generator
Electrically identical to IDG generators
Can power either or both main busses
May be used in flight as a replacement for an IDG source
APU Selection Priority
  If no other power source is available, APU generator automatically connects to both main AC busses
  If <u>primary external</u> is powering <u>both main busses,</u>
    APU powers left main AC bus
    Primary external source powers right main bus
  If <u>primary external</u> is powering the <u>right</u> main bus *AND*
    <u>Secondary external</u> is powering the <u>left</u> main bus, When APU comes on line it replaces the secondary and powers the <u>left main</u> bus
  If <u>secondary external</u> is powering <u>both main busses</u> when the APU comes on line, the APU will replace it and power both main busses
APU Generator Off Light indicates
  APU generator is operating, but the generator breaker is open due to either a fault *OR*
  APU Generator switch is selected **OFF**

Bus Tie Breaker Priorities
♦ Respective side
♦ APU
♦ Opposite Side

External Power
Two types of external connection
  Primary
  Secondary
  Either is capable of powering both main AC busses
  Some items will be load-shed due to capacity restrictions

Connecting power
  Different for primary and secondary
  Primary—**AVAIL** light will illuminate when primary external power is connected, regardless of other switch positions
  Secondary—**AVAIL** light only on when battery switch is **ON OR** primary power is available

AC Bus Power Distribution

Source/Bus	Normally Powers
Right IDG	R Main AC Bus
Left IDG	L Main AC Bus
Primary External (when connected)	R Main AC Bus
Secondary External (when connected)	L Main AC Bus
APU	Left or Both Unpowered Main AC Busses
R Main AC Bus	Ground Service Bus
APU Generator *OR* Primary External Power	Ground Handling Bus

        (*No other sources* can power this bus)

Main AC Bus (Each)	Respective **Transfer Bus**
	Respective **Utility Bus**
	Respective **Galley Bus**
Transfer Busses	**DC Transformer-Rectifiers**
	AC Standby Bus
Utility Busses	Forward Galley Heater, Chiller Boost fan

    Also: CA & FO Area Heaters, Lav Heaters & Shaver Outlets, Gasper Fan

Ground Service Bus	**Main & APU Battery Chargers**

    Also: Miscellaneous cabin and system loads, cabin lighting and outlets, Left forward fuel pump
Isolation for Autolandings occurs when:
  Approach mode is engaged and
  Aircraft passes through 1500' radio altitude

Auto-Pilot	Powered By
Captain	Left IDG through the
	L AC Transfer Bus and the
	L Main DC Bus and the
	Captain's Flight Instrument Bus
Center	Right IDG through the
	Main Battery Charger and the
	Battery Bus and the
	AC Standby Bus
First Officer	Backup System, which powers
	R AC Transfer Bus and the
	R Main DC Bus and the
	First Officer's Flight Instrument Bus

Electrical System Autoland Bus Isolation
(Selected Major Components)

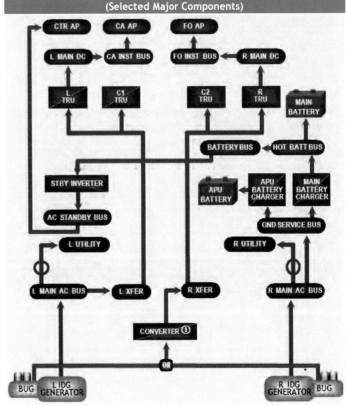

Backup AC Electrical System

Provides Power to Key Sub-Systems

Automatically activated when:
Only one main AC Generator available (including APU)
Power to one or both of the main AC busses is lost
Approach (**APP**) is selected for autoland
System is tested after engine starts

System transfers power without interruption

Components

Backup Generators (BUG)
One in each engine accessory drive
Not speed regulated (not constant speed)
Output is regulated to 400 Hz by a converter
Come on line and stay on line slightly below idle engine RPM
Converter
Receives input from both backup generators at all times engines are running
Can select and process inputs from only one BUG or the other, not both simultaneously
Permanent Magnet Generators (PMG)
Two contained in each BUG
Supply AC power to flight control Power Supply Assemblies (PSA)
PSAs convert power from AC to DC for flight control computer use
Output is dedicated to flight controls—cannot be diverted elsewhere

DC Electrical System

Key DC Components Powered by DC

Main DC Electrical System
◆ PFDs   ◆ NDs   ◆ GPS   ◆ ADIRU

Flight Control DC Electrical System

Transformer Rectifier Units (TRUs)

TRU	Powers/*Alternate For*	Backup From
L TRU	L Main DC Bus	Bus Tie to R
	L Flt Ctrl Bus	
	R Main DC Bus	
R TRU	R Main DC Bus	Bus Tie to L
	R Flt Ctrl Bus	
	L Main DC Bus	
C1 TRU	Captain's Flight Instrument Bus	Bus Tie to F/O
	Battery Bus	
	Hot Battery Bus	(*Through Battery Bus*)
	Standby Inverter	(*Through Hot Battery Bus*)
	Center Flight Control PSA	
	FO Flight Instrument Bus	
C2 TRU	First Officer's Flt Instrument Bus	Bus Tie to CA
	CA Flight Instrument Bus	

DC Busses

Hot Battery Bus—With battery switch off, powers 3 items
◆ Engine fire extinguisher bottles
◆ APU fire extinguisher bottle
◆ ADIRU, if switch is on

With only battery power available in flight, these systems are powered: Three items above, plus
◆ Standby Power System
◆ Captain's displays
◆ Left AIMS

Flight Control DC System—Designed to provide:
Dedicated and uninterrupted power to the primary flight control system PSAs
Primary power sources
Left and Right IDG Generators
Permanent Magnet Generators (PMGs)
Housed within backup generators
Dedicated power for flight control busses
Backup Power Sources
L and R Main DC Busses--can power alternate side Main DC Bus
Center Flight Control Bus
Alternate power—captain's flight instrument bus
Various power sources can power this bus

Hot Battery Bus can also provide power to left and center flight control bus
Individual Batteries
Connected to each flight control bus
Provide power for "short periods only" to insure no interruptions only during power transfers

Standby Electrical System

System Overview

Supplies AC and DC Power to selected key items
System Components
Main Battery
Standby Inverter
RAT Generator & associated generator control unit
C1 & C2 TRUs

Main Battery

Provides standby power to
◆ Hot Battery Bus   ◆ Left and Center Flight Control Busses
◆ Battery Bus   ◆ Captain's Flight Instrument Bus
◆ Standby Inverter, which powers the AC Standby Bus
Note: *Main battery can power the standby system for a minimum of 10 minutes*
Main Battery Charger
Powered by R Main DC Bus (through the Ground Service Bus)
When powered, the battery charger powers
Hot Battery Bus
L and Center Flight control busses
Battery Switch
ON—On the ground and not powered:
Some switch annunciator lights are illuminated
Allows the APU to be started.
On the ground after AC power is removed or lost:
Standby busses and emergency lighting are powered
The left inboard, outboard, and upper center displays, and the left CDU are powered.
OFF—On the ground, battery bus not powered and the EICAS advisory message **ELEC BATTERY OFF** is displayed
In flight, the EICAS advisory message **ELEC BATTERY OFF** is displayed.

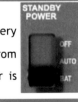

Standby Inverter

Converts DC to AC
Powers AC Standby Bus if L Transfer Bus is not powered

Standby Power Switch

Note: *Ground operation only*
OFF—The AC Standby Bus is not powered
AUTO (Guarded)—Standby Busses transfer to battery power if normal AC power is lost
BAT (Momentary)—Standby Busses are powered from the battery if AC power is not available
Initiates a DC / standby self-test if AC power is available.

Ram Air Turbine (RAT)

Provides Hydraulic Power to Center system flight controls
See Hydraulic system, *page 51* for details function hydraulic
No limits on time or speeds for deployment
Provides standby electrical power for
C1 & C2 TRUs
Priority is hydraulic pressure over electrical power generation
Power for standby system switches to Battery if RAT sheds electrical power generation

Power from RAT both Captain's and F/O's flight instrument busses are powered through C1 & C2 TRUs

RAT Deployment switch
Press—deploys RAT
UNLKD Light (*Amber*) indicates RAT is not in stowed position
PRESS Light (*Green*) indicates RAT is deployed and producing
≥ 1500psi

RAT Deploys if: (HEED)
  Hydraulic—All 3 hydraulic system pressures are low **OR**
  Electrical—Both AC transfer busses are unpowered **OR**
  Engines both fail **AND** center hydraulic pressure low **OR**
  Deployed manually

Acronyms

ELMS ....Electrical load management system
IDG ....Integrated drive generator
PSA Power Supply Assemblies
TRU ....Transformer Rectifier Unit

RAT Power plus Battery—Key cockpit items

Battery Only—Key cockpit items shaped in a "T"

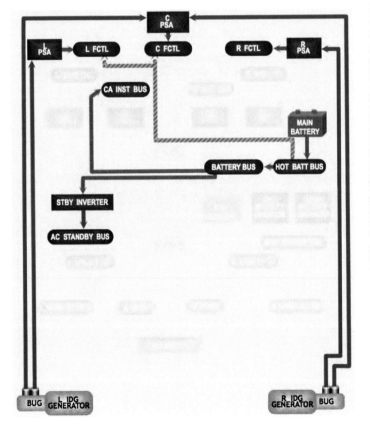

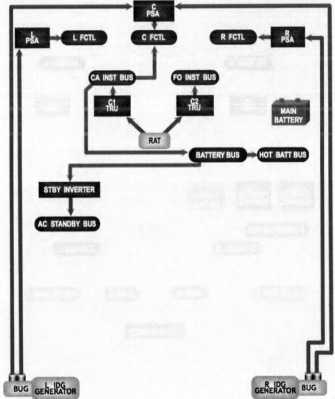

Engines

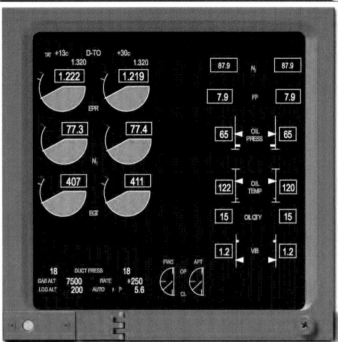

General Engine Characteristics

200ER Designation ....Rolls Royce Trent 892
Thrust Rating (each)............90,000 pounds at Takeoff Thrust
300ER Designation ....General Electric GE 90-115BL
Thrust Rating (each) ....115,000 pounds at Takeoff Thrust
Compressor-Turbines (3 Sections)
N_1–Rotor: Fan and low pressure turbine section on a common shaft
N_2–Rotor: Intermediate pressure compressor and turbine sections on a common shaft
200ER N_3–Rotor: High pressure compressor and turbine sections on a common shaft
Three sections are mechanically independent (**300ER** two sections)
N_3 Rotor drives engine accessory gearbox

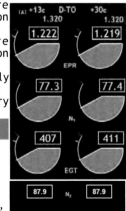

Engine Indications

Primary Engine Indications
200ER EPR, N_1, and EGT
300ER N1 and EGT
Displayed on EICAS by default
Secondary Indications
N_2, N_3, fuel flow, oil pressure, temperature & quantity, and vibration (**300ER** no N3)
Displayed on MFD with DSP **ENG** button
If MFD failure occurs, can display in compact format on EICAS
Automatic display of secondary indications commanded when any of the following occurs:
♦ Displays initially receive electrical power
♦ Fuel control switch moved to cutoff in flight
♦ Engine fire switch is pulled in flight
♦ Secondary parameter limit is exceeded
♦ N_3 RPM below idle in flight
When these conditions occur,

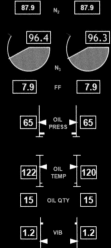

secondary display cannot be cleared until condition is no longer present
Abnormal Secondary Instrument Indications
Vibration Monitoring—indicates source (**N1, N2** or **N2**) or **BB** (broadband) if source can't be determined
Oil quantity Low—**LO** displayed and numbers reverse to black on white when low

Exceedance Indication
If amber band or red line exceedance conditions occur, indication box and pointer turn to red
When condition returns to normal range
Box remains red
Numbers return to white
DSP **CANC / RCL** button returns box to white

Electronic Engine Controls (EECs)

Full authority over engine operation
Uses thrust lever inputs to automatically control forward and reverse thrust
Two control modes
Normal—Uses EPR as primary thrust reference setting
300ER Uses N1 as primary thrust reference control
Alternate—Uses N1 RPM to set thrust
Maximum rated thrust is available in any phase of flight by moving thrust levers to the full forward positions
Alternate mode—selected automatically
Called "Soft" alternate
Switch is still in normal
A/T remains engaged
N1 becomes primary thrust controlling parameter

	Normal	Soft Alternate	Hard Alternate
	NORM	NORM / ALTN	ALTN
Indications	ALL	EPR: Blank N1: Actual Red Line	EPR: Blank N1: Actual Command Ref/Target Maximum Red Line
Thrust Ref N1	**300ER**	X	X
Thrust Ref EPR	**200ER**		
Thrust Limit (Over**boost**) Protection	X	**200ER** **300ER** Available with A/T **300ER** Available at full forward thrust lever	
Over**speed** Protection	X	X	X

(**X** Indicates feature is available)

Hard Alternate Mode—selected manually by pressing switch
No thrust limit protection
Reduce thrust before selecting
With autothrottle engaged, thrust limit protection returns
300ER **EEC Differences**
All three modes—actual, command, reference/target, maximum, and red line N1 information is displayed.
Automatic reversion or manual selection to alternate mode
Indicated by the
EICAS advisory message **ENG EEC MODE** (**L** or **R**) *AND*
EEC **ALTN** light on associated mode switch
Selecting alternate mode on both engines eliminates thrust lever stagger at equal thrust settings, or asymmetric thrust when thrust levers are operated together
Autothrottles remain engaged when EEC automatically switches to alternate mode.
FMC computes alternate mode N1 reference/target values
EICAS Advisory message **ENG RPM LIMITED** (**L** / **R**) provided when overspeed protection is active
Note: *Autothrottles remains engaged in soft or hard alternate mode*

EEC Idle Selection
EEC Selects approach idle or minimum idle automatically
Higher thrust for quicker engine response is provided with approach idle selection
Approach idle is selected in flight if:
- ♦ Engine anti-ice is operating
- ♦ Flaps in landing position (25 or 30°)
- ♦ One hydraulic air-driven demand pump is INOP, and the flaps are out of the UP position
- ♦ The opposite engine bleed air valve is closed

AutoStart
Normal start system
Start selectors control starter air valves
Fuel cutoff switches control ignition and fuel flow
EEC monitors start and commands start selectors to **NORM** and bleed air cut off at 50% N_3
Packs are shut off when start cycle begins and are automatically restarted after start cycle is complete

Start is aborted for	Restart OK	Ground, No Restart
Hot Start	★	
Hung Start	★	
No EGT Rise	★	
Compressor Stall	★	
Starter Shaft Failure		X
Air—Insufficient air pressure		X
N₁—No N₁ rotation		X
Duty—Start time exceeds starter duty cycle		X

★ *Restart attempts occur automatically for these items*

AutoStart is not aborted for
Oil pressure or oil temperature
These are **_not monitored_** by autostart
In-flight assisted autostarts
System temporarily discontinues the start *IF*
- ♦ T/O EGT red line limit is reached, *OR*
- ♦ No light-off *OR*
- ♦ Hung start is detected
For any of these, autostart system
- ♦ Windmills engine 30 seconds before next attempt
- ♦ Uses windmill motoring between attempts (starter is re-engaged on the following start attempt)
- ♦ Corrective action occurs automatically for unspecified "detected problems" without aborting start attempt
- ♦ During second and subsequent start attempts—autostart re-introduces fuel & ignition when EGT falls below 200°C

Thrust Control Malfunction Protection
Protects against high thrust malfunction on the ground
Shuts down engine when
- ♦ Airplane on ground *AND*
- ♦ Thrust lever at idle *AND*
- ♦ Engine above idle speed and not decelerating normally

EICAS warning message ENG FAIL (**L** or **R**) displays on PFD if
Thrust is less than commanded with
Airspeed between 65 knots and 6 knots prior to V1

EICAS caution message ENG FAIL (**L** or **R**) displays when engine speed reduces below idle speed
Remains displayed until fuel cutoff switch is in **CUTOFF**

EICAS caution Message ENG THRUST (**L** or **R**) displays when:
- ♦ Actual thrust is significantly less than commanded *OR*
- ♦ Actual thrust is not increasing to commanded thrust, *AND*
  Airspeed is greater than 6 knots below V₁

Autostart
ON - Arms the autostart system.
OFF - Switch **OFF**, Autostart system is disabled
Start must be manually controlled

Manual Starts
Autostart Switch OFF selects manual start mode
Fuel control switch should not be moved to **RUN** with EGT over 100°C ....See OM Volume I, Systems 45.3
OM Volume II, ENGINES, APU 7.20.12, 7.20.13

Engine Start Switches
START—Initiates engine start by opening the start valve
Releases to **NORM** at start valve cutout
NORM—The start valve closes
300ER CON—Both ignitors operate continuously (if the **FUEL CONTROL** switch is in **RUN**) when:
- ♦ On ground, N1 > approximately 55% N1 with takeoff flaps set, *OR*
- ♦ In flight

Engine Ignition
Two igniters
EEC Selects igniter for each start
Igniters are alternated on subsequent starts
In flight starts always use both igniters
Power sources
Normal—Main AC power
Backup—Standby AC (Standby inverter)

Auto Relight Function
Activates below idle with fuel control switches in **RUN**
Continues until engine spools down to down to 35% N_3
If system is deactivated due to N_3 below 35%
It may be reenergized by moving fuel cutoff to **CUTOFF** and back to **RUN**
This is the reason for the **Red Box** procedure
Flameout protection provided in heavy hail/rain
300ER Differences
EEC-Detected flameout—both ignitors activate
Sub-idle stall detection—fuel shut off for one second to clear stall then fuel restarts

Engine Fuel System
200ER Fuel path to engine
- ♦ Fuel flows through a spar valve located in the respective main tank
- ♦ Engine stage fuel pump increases pressure
- ♦ Preheating occurs in an engine-oil heat exchanger
- ♦ A fuel filter removes contaminants
- ♦ A second fuel pump further increases pressure
- ♦ Fuel is metered in accordance with commanded thrust
- ♦ Fuel flows last through the engine fuel valve before reaching the injectors

Both fuel valves close when
The fire switch is pulled *or*
The engine fuel control switch is moved to **CUTOFF**

300ER Fuel path slightly different
Spar valve through engine stage fuel pump same as above, then:
- ♦ A second fuel pump further increases pressure
- ♦ Preheating occurs in an engine-oil heat exchanger
- ♦ A fuel filter removes contaminants

Fuel metering and remaining path to engine is the same as above for -200 series engines
Diagrams ....OMV2, ENGINES, APU 7.20.19 to 7.20.20

Fuel Control Switches
RUN (Autostart ON)—Opens spar fuel valve
Arms engine fuel valve (EEC opens valve when required)
Arms selected ignitor(s)
EEC turns ignitors on when required
RUN (Autostart OFF)—
Opens spar fuel valve
Opens engine fuel valve
Turns ignitors on
CUTOFF
Closes the fuel valves
Removes ignitor power
Unlocks the Engine Fire Switch

Engine Oil System

The engine oil system lubricates and cools
Engine main bearings
Gears & accessory drives
The system provides
Fuel heating
Fuel system icing protection
No Minimum oil quantity (amber or red line limit)
Low oil quantity causes automatic display of secondary engine indications
Reverses display to show quantity in black on white background
300ER Oil Filter Clogging
If filter clogs, it is bypassed
EICAS advisory message **ENG OIL FILTER** (**L** or **R**) is displayed

Thrust Reversers

Hydraulically operated
Use system pressure from respective side hydraulic system
Levers can only be raised when
On the ground
Thrust Levers are at idle
When reverse levers are pulled aft to the interlock position:
Autothrottle disengages
Auto speed brakes deploy
When reverse is terminated, thrust levers cannot be advanced until reverse levers are fully down
EICAS advisories
Advisory message **ENG REV LIMITED** (**L** or **R**)
Reverser cannot deploy when commanded or will be limited to idle
Not all conditions detectable
If other limiting conditions, thrust levers simply restricted to idle reverse
Advisory message **ENG REVERSER** (**L** or **R**)
Displayed on ground to indicate reverser system fault
Note: **200ER** *Following any rejected takeoff where thrust reversers were deployed, maintenance must determine if an inspection of the thrust reversers is necessary prior to the next takeoff.* .... *QRH LANDING GEAR 14.5*

Engine Failure Alert

Triggered when engine produces less than commanded thrust
Message ENG FAIL is displayed (*Red*) on PFD if
Actual thrust is less than commanded and
Speed is between 65 knots and V_1
Message ENG FAIL L or **R** is displayed (*Caution*) on EICAS if engine decelerates to less than idle speed
Remains displayed until:
Engine thrust recovers *or*
Fuel control switch is moved to **CUTOFF**
Message ENG THRUST L or **R** is displayed (*Caution*) on EICAS if
Actual thrust is significantly less than commanded *and*
Actual thrust is not increasing *and*
Speed is between 65 knots and 6 knots below V_1

APU—Auxiliary Power Unit General

Priorities
Electrical power *then*
Bleed Air
Operating Envelope
Can operate and provide electric power throughout aircraft envelope
Bleed air only available to 22,000' pressure altitude

Starting

Two starting systems
Air turbine starter
Uses engine bleed air or ground cart air
Electric motor starter
Powered by APU battery
Main airplane battery powers
Inlet door
Fuel valve
Fire detection system
Starter selection is automatic
Bleed air start is used if available

Fuel

Supply is from left main fuel manifold
Left forward AC fuel boost pump operates continuously to provide fuel if
AC power is available *and*
APU Selector on
(*Regardless of boost pump switch position*)
For APU starting and running when only DC power is available, a DC pump in the left main tank operates
APU Shuts down automatically if start attempt fails
In Flight Automatic Start occurs when Both AC transfer busses lose power
APU Starts regardless of switch position
May be shut down by moving selector to **ON**, then **OFF**
In-Flight Start Reliability Program
Selected flights—crews requested to attempt in flight start after 2 hours at cruise altitude
Maximum attempts if unsuccessful start—two additional attempts (three total attempts)
Reliability improvement
Place Start Switch in **ON** for one minute before start
Allows start logic to complete before selecting **START**
Allows APU inlet door to fully open
Momentarily hold start switch in **START**

APU Shutdown

APU Cool down cycle begins automatically when selector is moved to **OFF**
Cycle lasts 105 seconds under a no-load condition
If APU Selector is moved back to RUN within the cool down cycle, APU stays running
APU must slow to below 12% before restart can be initiated

APU Operating Modes

Attended Mode—Definition
Either engine running or starting *or*
Airplane in flight

APU Shuts down for any of these faults with no cool down period
♦ APU Fire or inlet over temperature
♦ Overspeed or loss of speed protection
♦ APU controller failure
♦ Speed droop

EICAS Advisory message **APU SHUTDOWN** displays
Note: *Previous OM versions describe a speed drop as RPM <88% and no acceleration for 10 seconds*
APU Continues to operate with these faults:
♦ High EGT
♦ High oil temperature
♦ Low oil pressure

Following these faults, there is no cool down when the APU is shut down
For any of these, EICAS caution message **APU LIMIT** displays
Unattended Mode Definition
On ground, with no engines running or starting

Shutdown occurs automatically for any of the faults above, plus:
♦ Generator oil filter approaching bypass
♦ Intake door failure
♦ No combustion on start
♦ No acceleration on start
No cool down period for any of these prior to shutdown

EICAS Advisory message **APU SHUTDOWN** displays

APU Fuel Usage

Approximately 600 pounds per hour
See OMV1, Systems-45.2

Acronyms

EICAS .... Engine indicating and crew alerting system
EEC .... Engine electronic controller
EPR .... Engine pressure ratio
MFD .... Multifunction Display

Fire Protection

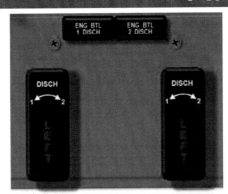

APU Fire Detection results in APU automatic shutdown
> If APU is unattended, single APU fire bottle also discharges automatically
> APU considered unattended with the airplane on the ground if engines are not running or starting

Fire Warnings

Fire detection results in:
> Aural Warnings
> > ♦ Fire warning bell (intermittent)
> > Fire Warning Messages and Lights
> > ♦ Both Master **WARNING** lights come ON
> > ♦ EICAS Warning messages
> > > `ENG FIRE L` and `ENG FIRE R`
> > > `FIRE APU`
> > ♦ Affected Fuel Control Fire light ON (*Red*)
> > ♦ Affected fire switch ON (*Red*) for engines or APU
> > Mechanical Changes
> > ♦ Affected fire switch unlock for engines or APU
> APU Only
> > ♦ APU Shutdown for APU fire (attended **or** unattended mode)
> > ♦ Nose strut mounted fire warning horn if on ground
> > ♦ Fire bottle automatically released if APU fire signal is generated with engines not running or being started (unattended mode)

Overheat Cautions
Aural Warning—Caution beeper sounds
Fire Warning Messages and Lights
> ♦ EICAS—Caution message `OVERHEAT ENG L` or `R`
Both Master **CAUTION** lights
> ♦ EICAS message remains on until overheat condition is terminated

Fire Bottles

Eight Total, / `300ER`**, Nine Total**
> 2: Engines
> 5: Cargo compartments / `300ER`, 6 in cargo compartments
> 1: APU
Two provided for use in engines
> Either or both can be discharged into either engine
> Pulling Engine Fire Switch
> > Arms discharge squib on each bottle
> Rotating Switch
> > Selects the bottle to be used **and**
> > Discharges it into the associated engine
> Rotating Switch in Opposite Direction
> > Selects the opposite bottle **and**
> > Discharges it into the same engine
One for APU
> Manual discharge
> > Pulling APU Fire Switch arms bottle for discharge
> > Rotating switch in either direction discharges bottle into APU compartment
> Automatic Discharge
> > Occurs with airplane on the ground and engines not running or being started
> > Discharge occurs a few seconds after APU automatic shutdown

If a bottle discharges or has low pressure:
ENG BTL 1 or **2 DISCH** light illuminates
EICAS Advisory message **BOTTLE 1** or **2 DISCH ENG**

> `ENG BTL 1 DISCH`

General

Fire Protection and Overheat Detection

Component	Fire Detection	Extinguishing System	Overheat detection
Both Engines	X	X	X
APU	X	X	
Cargo Compartment	X	X	
Lavatories	X	X	
FD Crew Rest Area	X		
Main Deck Crew Rest Area	X		
`300ER` Upper Deck Crew Rest Areas	X		
Main Wheel Wells	X		

Power Sources

Unlike other aircraft—Power sources for fire protection / detection not specified nor emphasized in OMV2 or in ground school
QRH does not include lists of inoperative systems
Sufficient redundancy exists to protect fire-related systems

Engine & APU Fire/Overheat Protection

Fire & Overheat Detector Loops

Dual loops on each engine, the APU, and in wheel wells
> Engines only—loops provide both fire and overheat detection
Normal operation—both loops must detect fire for warning activation
Loop Fault
> Single loop failure—Switch to single loop sensing occurs
> > Fire detected in remaining loop results in fire `WARNING` or overheat `CAUTION` activation
> Double loop failure—EICAS advisory message `DET FIRE ENG L` or `R` results

Wheel Well Fire Protection

Dual detector loops
Main Wheel wells only (not nose gear well)
No fire protection provided

Lavatory Detection

`200ER` `SMOKE LAVATORY` EICAS advisory message displays
`300ER` `SMOKE LAV/COMP` EICAS advisory message displays

Cargo Compartment Fire Protection

Smoke Detection

Both forward and aft cargo compartments divided into three zones

If **smoke** detected in any zone, **fire warning** results for that compartment

If detection system is inoperative, EICAS advisory message results DET FIRE CARGO FWD or AFT

200ER Three detection zones

300ER Four detection zones

Cargo Fire Switches

Armed (pushed)

Key Items (*Arms, Aims, Air*):

Arms all cargo fire extinguisher bottles

Aims—Arms selected compartment extinguisher valve

Air—Reduced flow
- Turns off both lower recirculation fans
- Shuts down cargo heat
- Commands packs to low flow (minimum air flow required to provide pressurization)
- **300ER** Shuts down Nitrogen Generation System

Aft cargo fire only:
Shuts down bulk cargo compartment ventilation system operation
Shuts down the lavatory & galley vent fan

Forward cargo fire only: Puts the equipment cooling system into the override mode

DISCH Switch

Discharges cargo fire suppression into armed compartment

DISCH light in switch—fire extinguishers have discharged

Fire Warning

Indications of fire include:
Fire bell
Master **WARNING** light
EICAS Warning message **FIRE CARGO FWD** or **AFT**
CARGO FIRE FWD or **AFT** Fire warning light

Fire Extinguishing

200ER Five fire bottles provided

300ER Six fire bottles provided

In flight fire extinguishing

Pressing the appropriate cargo fire discharge switch:
- Activates a small explosive charge (squib)
- Sound is a muffled explosive sound in the cabin
- Two bottles are discharged fully into the affected compartment
- After a time delay*
  - If still airborne, remaining three bottles are discharged at a reduced rate
  - If landing occurs, but aircraft is not shut down
    Only 1 bottle is discharged at touchdown *and*
    Discharge is at a reduced rate

Ground fire extinguishing

Pressing the cargo fire discharge switch:
- Activates a small explosive charge (squib) as above
- Two bottles are discharged fully into the affected compartment
- After a time delay* if the aircraft is still not shut down, only 1 bottle is discharged (no metering)

***Note:** Older versions of the operating manual identified the time delay as 20 minutes*

Fire System Tests and Controls

Fire / Overheat System Tests

Automatic

Occurs at initial power up
Continuous tests of loops occur while electrical power is applied
Fault notification through EICAS is provided

Manual Test

Accomplished by pressing and holding the Fire / Overheat Test Switch

---

Manual Test Indications:

Interior—1 Red EICAS message, **9** Red lights, fire bell
- EICAS FIRE TEST IN PROG ....1 Red
- Changes to FIRE TEST PASS or FIRE TEST FAIL when complete
- Master **WARNING** (2)............................2 Red
- L and R Engine Fire Handles Light.....................2 Red
- APU Fire Switch Light ....1 Red
- FWD and AFT Cargo Fire Warning Lights.............2 Red
- Left and Right Fuel Control Switch Fire Lights.......2 Red
- Fire Bell .... Total: 10 Red

Exterior—1 Light, Fire Horn
- Nose Wheel Well APU Fire Warning Light.............1 Red
- Nose wheel well APU fire warning horn (on ground)

Engine Fire Handles

Normal position—in and locked

Switch unlock occurs for:
Fire warning
Fuel control switch in cutoff
Override button is pressed

When pulled, the following actions take place:
- Arms engine fire extinguisher bottles
- Closes associated engine and spar fuel valve
- Closes associated bleed air valve
- Trips associated engine generator off
- Shuts off hydraulic fluid to engine-driven hydraulic pump
- Depressurizes respective engine-driven hydraulic pump
- Removes power to thrust reverser isolation valve

Rotated Left or **Right**—Discharges fire bottle 1 or 2 into respective engine

Engine Fire Switch Override Switch
Button under switch
Allows release of switch if electrical lock does not release

Engine bottle Discharged Light
Indicates extinguisher bottle is discharged *or*
Low bottle pressure

Fuel Control Fire Warning Lights
Associated fire detected *or*
Fire / Overheat Test Switch is Pressed

APU Fire Switch

Above applies to APU as well, except:
Only one fire bottle
Rotating switch either direction discharges single APU fire extinguisher bottle
APU is shut down automatically on fire warning, not when switch is pulled
Pulling the switch shuts down the APU if auto shutdown fails to do so for any reason

On the ground with both engines shut down
APU fire signal from either fire detection loop causes
- APU Shutdown *and*
- Extinguisher bottle discharge

Flight Controls

Flight Control Synoptic

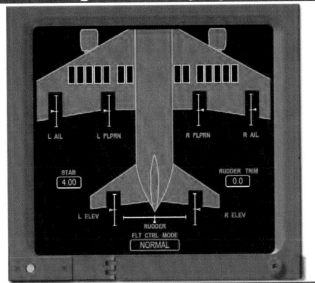

Flight Control Modes

Normal Mode

Designed mode for all operations

Flight control inputs command these system electronic components:
- Four actuator control electronics units (ACEs)
- Three primary flight computers (PFCs)

Manual Flight
- Pilot inputs sent to the four ACEs
- ACEs send these signals to the three PFCs
- PFCs verify signals and information from other airplane systems to compute control surface commands
- Commands are sent back to ACEs
- ACEs send enhanced signals to the flight control surface actuators

Autopilot Flight
- Autopilot sends signals to the PFCs
- PFCs generate control surface commands and send these to the ACEs
- ACEs then operate as above
- Signals are generated to move yoke and rudder pedals to reflect commanded motion of flight controls
- If pilot inputs override autopilot commands, A/P is disconnected and pilot inputs are used
- Autopilot flight only available in *normal mode*

Secondary Mode

Entering Secondary Mode
- Occurs when PFCs can no longer support normal mode
- Causes may include:
  - ◆ Internal faults
  - ◆ Lack of required information from other airplane systems
  - ◆ Reversion to secondary mode then occurs automatically
- *Secondary mode cannot be manually selected*

Command to Flight Controls
- ACEs continue to receive pilot inputs on yoke and rudder pedals
- Signals sent to PFCs use simplified computations to generate flight control surface commands
- Simplified commands are returned to ACEs
- ACEs generate commands sent to flight control actuators

Flight Characteristics
- All flight controls surfaces remain operable
- Elevator and rudder are more sensitive "at some airspeeds"

Autopilot—Not available

EICAS Message
- FLIGHT CONTROL MODE Caution message and beeper
- Indicates flight controls are in secondary mode

Direct Mode

Entering Direct Mode
- ACEs transition to direct mode when
  - They detect the failure of all three PFCs *or*
  - They lose communication with the PFCs
- Manual selection of direct mode
  - Primary Flight Control Computer Disconnect switch to **DISC** selects direct mode

EICAS Message
- PRI FLIGHT COMPUTERS Caution message and beeper
- Indicates flight controls are in direct mode

Flight Characteristics
- PFCs no longer generate control surface commands
- Pilot inputs are routed through ACEs directly to the control surface actuators
- Full airplane control is available for "continued safe flight and landing"
- Airplane handling qualities are "approximately the same as in secondary mode"

Mechanical Backup

Mode Design
- In event of complete electrical failure, direct connection to flight controls
- Cables from flight deck to stabilizer and two spoilers (4 & 11)
- Stabilizer control
  - Cable connected from alternate pitch trim levers mechanically connect to valves on each stabilizer trim control module
  - Hydraulic fluid directed to actuator to move stabilizer
- Spoilers
  - Control wheel mechanically controls spoilers 4 and 11
  - Direct cable connection from both yokes to actuators on these spoilers
- Yaw control
  - May be available through differential thrust

Flight Characteristics—Mode allows pilot to *"fly straight and level until the electrical system is restarted"*

Primary Flight Computer Disconnect Switch

DISC—Disconnects the primary flight computers (PFCs) from the flight control system
- Puts flight control system in the direct mode

AUTO—Normal position—Flight control system in **Normal** mode
- System faults automatically cause system to switch to secondary or direct modes.
- Reselection may allow restoration of secondary or normal mode operation

DISC Light—Indicates PFCs are disconnected (either manually or automatically)

Flight Mode Capabilities

Mode	Normal	Secondary	Direct
All normal & automatic features	X		
Yaw Damping	X	Some	
Manual Rudder Trim Cancel	X	X	
Rudder Ratio	X	Degraded	Degraded
Elevator Feel	X	Degraded	Degraded

Flight Envelope Protection

Stall Protection

Limits speed to which airplane may be trimmed
- At approximately minimum maneuvering speed, further trim inhibited toward slower speed (nose up)
- Pilot must apply back pressure to maintain slower speed
- Alternate pitch trim switches do not override this inhibit
- Flying near stall speed, aft yoke movement requires increasing force

Autothrottle Protection

If: .Autothrottle is armed and not engaged, **and**
....Speed decreases to near stick shaker activation
Then: Autothrottle engages in the SPD mode **and**
  Advances thrust to maintain **the greater of**:
    Minimum maneuvering speed (*equates to near top of amber band*) **or**
    Speed set in MCP window
  Autothrottle protection/engagement is inhibited:
    Pitch control in TOGA or FLCH **or**
    Below 400' above airport on takeoff **or**
    Below 100' radio altitude on approach

Overspeed Protection

Limits speed to which airplane can be trimmed
Nose down trim is inhibited at V_{MO} / M_{MO}
Alternate pitch trim switches do not override this inhibit

Roll Envelope Bank Protection

Activates when airplane bank angle exceeds ≈35°, 40° and 45°
300ER Also sounds low altitude during takeoff and landing for bank angles as small as 10°
Result—Control wheel force rolls airplane back to within 30° bank angle
Limits on protection
  Can be overridden by pilot
  Full yoke deflection always results in full control surface displacement
  Autopilot disengage bar disables bank angle protection
Indications
  Excessive bank indicated on PFD bank indicator
  Color changes to amber on both roll and slip/skid indications when 35° roll is exceeded. ....See OMV2, FLT-I p. 64

Other Flight Control Features

Thrust Asymmetry Compensation

Engages when **thrust** differential between engines is ≥10%
Available at all times except when:
  Airspeed below 70 knots on the ground **or**
  Reverse thrust applied **or**
  Flight controls are in secondary or direct mode **or**
  Automatically disengaged due to
    System malfunction **or**
    Loss of engine thrust data
TAC Disengages when:
  Engine thrust data is lost **or**
  Engine is damaged or surges
TAC may cause some rudder pedal deflection just before it disengages
Before liftoff—reduced compensation to allow pilot cues through roll and yaw

THRUST
ASYM COMP

AUTO
OFF

Wheel-Rudder Crosstie

Allows control-wheel only inputs to control initial effects of engine failure
Control wheel inputs deflect rudder up to 8°
Maintains sideslip capability consistent with crosswind landing requirements
Operation
  ♦ In flight only
  ♦ Speed < 210 KIAS
  ♦ Normal flight control mode only

Yaw Damping

Inputs rudder commands to accomplish three things
  ♦ Counteract tendency of swept-wing aircraft to Dutch roll
  ♦ Coordinate turns
  ♦ Gust suppression
    Reduces effect of lateral gusts
    Improves ride quality
No controls or indicators

Rudder & Aileron Trim Panel

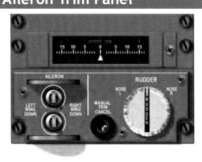

Stabilizer Trim

Actuation of both trim switches on either yoke:
  Normal mode on ground—moves stabilizer directly
  Normal mode in flight—changes trim reference airspeed
  Secondary & direct modes—moves stabilizer directly
Stabilizer trim green band
  Indicates allowable T/O trim range
  Inputs—Gross weight, T/O Thrust, CG
  If no inputs available from FMC—defaults to midrange
  Stab signal invalid or not present—green band and pointer not displayed
Stabilizer Trim Cutout Switches
  Respective C or R hydraulic power to the related stabilizer control module cut off

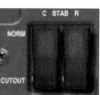

Flaps and Slats

Overview of Flap / Slat Positions

Flap Handle	Slats	Flaps	Range	Load Relief Primary Mode	Load Relief Secondary Mode
Up	Retract	Up			
1		Up			
5	Mid	5▯	T/O		
15		15▯			
20		20▯		Flap Relief	
25	Full	25▯	Land		Slat Relief
30		30▯			

Flap and Slat Mode Comparison

Flaps and slats may be in separate modes
Flap Modes—PSA
  Primary
  Secondary
  Alternate

Secondary Mode Entry

Occurs whenever primary mode fails to move slats or flaps to the selected position
Causes include:
  Loss of center system hydraulic pressure
  Flap component malfunctions
Restoration of primary mode
  Restoration of center hydraulic pressure
  Retraction of affected system surface(s) resets logic

Alternate Mode Entry

Occurs when Flap-Slat Electronic Units (FSEUs) are inoperative **and**
  Flaps and slats can no longer operate in the primary or secondary modes
Uses secondary drive motors
EICAS message **FLAP / SLAT CONTROL**
Manually entered with **ALTN** Switch
  Arms alternate flap control mode
  Arms Alternate Flaps Selector
  Disables primary and secondary flap / slat mode operation
  Inoperative:
  ♦ Flap / slat load relief ♦ Flap Handle
  ♦ Asymmetry / skew protection ♦ Autoslat
  ♦ Uncommanded motion protection

ARM
ALTN
OFF
RET   EXT

Flap / Slat Placard

On Landing Gear Panel

200ER FLAP LIMIT		300ER FLAP LIMIT	
1	255K	1	265K
5	235K	5	245K
15	215K	15	230K
20	195K	20	220K
25	185K	25	200K
30	170K	30	180K

Mode capabilities

Mode	Primary	Secondary	Alternate
Activation	Normal operation	Automatically engaged	Manually engaged
Flap & Slat Positioning	Hydraulic	Electrical	Electrical
FSEUs	Control movement	Control movement	Bypassed
Indication	Flaps & Slats Primary	Slats Primary, Flaps Secondary	Flaps & Slats Alternate
Protection Features	◆Autoslats ◆Flap load relief ◆Asymmetry protection ◆Uncommanded motion protection	◆Slats to full down at flaps 1° ◆Slat load relief ◆If slats in mid range at point of failure, remain in mid range until flaps retracted to up or extended beyond 20°	◆None ◆Max flap extension 20 ◆Slats to sealed (midrange) ext.

Loss of position information—displayed as a white outline with no tape fill and no flap lever position indication

After normal retraction—10 seconds after full retraction, indication is removed from EICAS

Load Relief

Primary Mode—Flap Relief
Protects against excessive aero forces due to overspeed
With flaps in 15-30° settings, if placard speed exceeded
LOAD RELIEF Memo message appears
Flaps retract to appropriate setting for speed
Minimum retraction setting is 5°
When speed decreases, flaps return to lower position, (no lower than handle set position)
If flaps selected above placard speed
Flaps remain in safe range until speed decreases
Flaps then are lowered to selected range
Flap handle is not moved to reflect relief position
Secondary Mode—Slat Relief
If airspeed over 239 knots **200ER** / 256 knots **300ER** with slats down (gapped) *OR*
Slats are retracted to midrange (sealed) position
LOAD RELIEF Memo message is displayed
Flaps must be retracted to full up to reset once this feature is activated
Inadvertent deployment—Cruise deployment above <u>altitude</u> approximately 20,000' is inhibited, *OR* <u>speed</u> above
200ER 265 knots
300ER 275 knots

Landing Flap Settings

Normal—Flaps 25 or 30
Several abnormal procedures—flaps 20
Flaps 25 preferred normally due to:
♦ Fuel efficiency (saves ≈14 gallons of fuel per landing)
♦ Noise abatement
♦ Reduced flap wear
♦ During high (gusty) wind conditions.
Note *The 777 is not certified for flaps 25 autoland.*
Flaps 30 recommended when landing with:
♦ <u>Runway</u>
Short runway (less than 8000 feet)
Slippery: Braking action reported less than good
Contaminated: Wet / contaminated runway, or
♦ <u>Weather</u>: Tailwind
♦ **Deemed prudent by the Captain.**
OMV1, Approach—Landing—Go-Around 10.1

Uncommanded Flap or Slat Motion

Uncommanded motion is detected when the slats or flaps:
♦ Move away from the commanded position *OR*
♦ Continue to move after reaching a commanded position *OR*
♦ Move in a direction opposite to that commanded
If the flap or slat is operating in the primary mode:
♦ Uncommanded motion causes automatic transfer to the secondary mode
♦ EICAS message caution **FLAPS PRIMARY FAIL** or **SLATS PRIMARY FAIL** is displayed.
♦ If motion continues, the system shuts down
♦ Resulting The EICAS message: **FLAPS DRIVE** or **SLATS DRIVE**

Spoilers

Location and naming
7 Sets of spoilers—(7 on each wing)
Numbered 1-14, L to R across aircraft wings
Symmetrically paired on opposing wings
Panels divided among the three hydraulic systems
EICAS advisory message **SPOILERS** indicates a pair has failed
Differential deployment aids roll control

> Autospoilers
> <u>Armed</u> when handle placed in **ARMED** position inflight
> <u>Activated</u> when:
> Gear on ground (not tilted) *AND* thrust levers both **IDLE** OR
> Either thrust lever moved to reverse **IDLE** detent

Speed Brake Use

Used to increase drag and decrease lift
Airborne use
Primary flight control mode—panels 5 & 10 locked out
In secondary and direct modes—panels 4, 5, 10 and 11 are locked out
Protects inboard ailerons

> **Speed brake deployment on landing**
> Occurs when all of the following are met:
> ♦ Speed brake handle is **ARMED**
> ♦ Thrust Levers are both idle
> ♦ Gear is not tilted
> <u>Also occurs</u> if A/C is on the ground (tilt sensed) and either reverse thrust lever is raised, regardless of speed brake and thrust lever condition

When armed, EICAS memo message, **SPEEDBRAKE ARMED**
Either thrust lever advanced to takeoff range causes handle to drive forward and retract speedbrake

Auto Slats

Stall warning system generates signal to autoslat system
Slats automatically extend
From mid-range, **TO** position (sealed)
To down (gapped) landing position
Slats retract "a few seconds after" signal is removed
System arming
Armed in 1, 5, 15 and 20° positions
Available only in
Primary slat mode *and*
When slats are in the sealed position

Flight Control Hydraulic Power Shutoff Switch Panel

Overhead panel—Primarily for maintenance use
No pilot procedures use these circuit shutoff switches

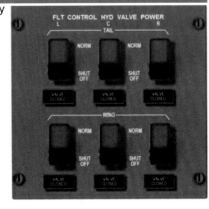

Flight Instruments

Note: *No attempt has been made here to completely describe the flight instrumentation displays and their connection to the FMS. These subjects are best learned using computer-aided color presentations, and are used on a day-to day basis by flight crews. Instead, key systems-related subjects have been summarized, which are easily forgotten and little used except for orals and recurrent training, and, of course, in the event of an actual malfunction. This section also serves as an overview for the transitioning crewmember.*

Displays

Six Liquid Crystal Display Units

Identical hardware

Display four primary types of information
- Primary flight display (PFD)
  - Displayed on outboard pilot station sides
  - Cannot be moved to other display units except in failure
- Navigation display (ND)
  - Normally displayed on inboard display positions
  - Can be displayed on lower center display
- Engine indicating and crew alerting system (EICAS)
  - Normally displayed on upper center position
  - Can be displayed on inboard or lower center positions
- Multifunction display (MFD)
  - Most commonly used position is lower center
  - Displays various information including
    - Electronic checklist
    - System synoptic
    - Communications information
    - Maintenance and other displays

Selection and Control
- ND information controlled by Electronic Flight Information System (EFIS) control panel on respective side
- If ND information is displayed on the lower center position, format is controlled by pilot whose inboard display position does ***not*** have ND displayed
- If neither pilot has navigation information displayed on their inboard display, then the left EFIS control panel controls the lower center ND information display
- If both pilots have ND displayed on inboard sides, and center ND is also displayed, left EFIS controls lower center panel and it is identical with left ND

Display Select Panel

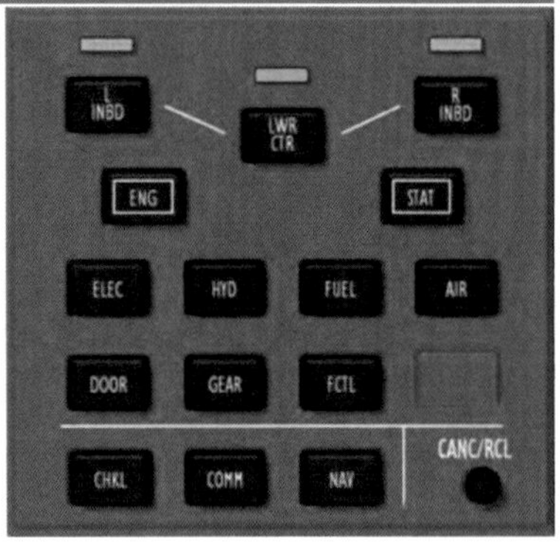

Controls MFD format on left and right inboard and center lower display units

Upper buttons (green indicator lights) select where information will appear

Center two rows of buttons select system synoptic displays

Lower row of buttons selects checklist, communications, or navigation display

A second push of the same button blanks the active display

300ER **CAM** button is placed in blank position at right to activate ground maneuver camera system

New information replaces previous display if a new button is selected

If panel fails, displays can be controlled through any CDU
- CDU capability exists at all times
- If activated, disables respective EFIS panel
- Only one CDU at a time can control an MFD

If an inboard display selector is in EICAS position
- Only **ENG**, **AIR** and **FUEL** switches can affect the display
- These buttons cause compacted information for respective systems to be displayed on bottom of display

If a PFD (outboard) display fails
- PFD is displayed on respective side inboard position
- Display select panel cannot control that position
- Selection of information on respective DSP brings up information requested on lower center position

If Upper Center display fails
- EICAS information is automatically displayed on lower center position display
- If EICAS information is then selected to an inboard display position
  - Lower center EICAS displays secondary engine indications
  - Lower display can then be used normally as long as EICAS information is displayed on one of the inboard displays

Electronic Flight Information System (EFIS) Control Panels

Select display options, mode and range for respective PFDs and NDs

If panel fails, displays can be controlled through respective CDU
- Display with **<MENU> <DSP CTL>** entries
- CDU capability exists at all times
- If activated, disables respective EFIS panel

Display Brightness Control

Master brightness control provides simultaneous adjustment of all displays and control lighting

Individual brightness knobs
- Control brightness within a span when master brightness control is ***on***
- Control brightness in the full possible range for that display or panel with master brightness control ***off***

Instrument Display Source Selection

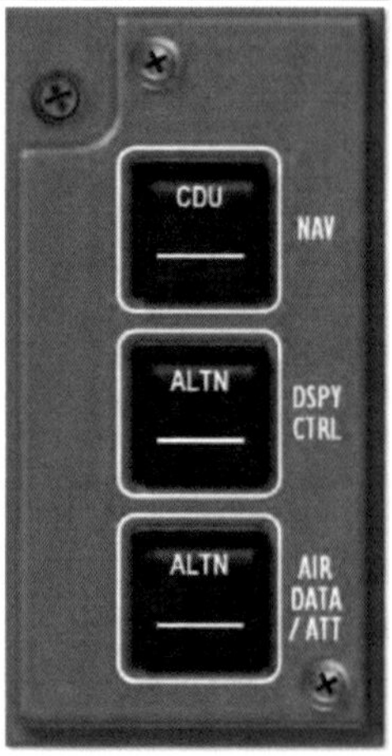

Display system automatically reconfigures for most failures

Source select switches provide alternate information sources for PFDs and NDs
- Automatic source selection occurs with switches off
  - This is switch out
  - **ALTN** and **CDU** switch annunciations not displayed

NAV Source Switch
- **OFF** (not depressed) Selects Auto
  - Active FMC provides data for ND map
  - ND Auto source—respective CDU
  - Right ND Auto
- **CDU** (**CDU** visible, depressed)
  - Selected CDU generates ND map

Display Control Source Switch
- **OFF** (not depressed) Selects Auto
  - Selects display processing channels for respective side outboard and inboard displays
  - Automatically reconfigures channels as required for display processing channel failures
- **ALTN** (**ALTN** visible, depressed)
  - Selects alternate source for current display processing channel

Air Data/Attitude Control Source Switch
- **OFF** (not depressed) Selects ADIRU for air data and attitude information to the PFD and ND
  - Alternate sources or SAARU are automatically selected to replace ADIRU air data or attitude, as required
- **ALTN** (**ALTN** visible, depressed)
  - Selects alternate source for PFD and ND as follows:
    - Air data (CA side): ....SAARU single channel
    - Air data (FO side): ....ADIRU single channel
    - Attitude (both sides): ....SAARU

Undetected source failures (part of display missing or incorrect)
- Switches allow pilot to select alternate source manually

Center display control source switch is provided below center display
- Same logic as **DSPL CTRL** source switch is used for center upper and lower display units

Standby Flight Instruments

Standby Attitude Indicator

SAARU attitude information is displayed
Bank indicator and **pitch scale** only
No FD display is possible

Standby Airspeed Indicator

Current airspeed displayed digitally in a box
Information calculated from two standby air data modules
    One module for pitot
    One module for static

Standby Altimeter

Displays altitude information from standby (static) air data module
Current altitude displayed digitally
Pointer indicates altitude in hundreds of feet
    One revolution is 1,000 feet

Standby Magnetic Compass

Liquid damped, standby compass on center upper windscreen brace
Heading correction information is on attached card

Clocks

Display airplane information management system (AIMS) generated:
    ♦ UTC time and date from GPS *OR*
    ♦ Manually set time and date
Can also display
    Alternating day and month-year
    Elapsed time and chronograph functions
AIMS UTC time information comes from GPS

Integrated Standby Flight Display (ISFD)

The **ISFD** (some airplanes) displays:
    ♦ Attitude   ♦ ILS
    ♦ Airspeed   ♦ Magnetic heading information
    ♦ Altitude
Power source is left flight control DC bus
Data sources
    Pitot-Static—Center
    Air Data—Standby modules
    Altitude, attitude, and airspeed are independent of ADIRU and SAARU values.
Attitude Reset Switch must be reset on the ground while airplane is stationary

Display System Information Sources

Air Data Inertial Reference System (ADIRS)

Information provided for:
    Primary, secondary and standby air data
    Inertial reference information
Major Components

        Note: *Engine inlets each have independent TAT probes not discussed here*

Air Data Inertial Reference Unit (ADIRU)

Primary source for following information:
    ♦ Speed   ♦ Altitude
    ♦ Attitude   ♦ Inertial navigation position
Processes information measured by
    Inertial gyros and accelerometers
    Its own air data module inputs
    AOA vanes
    Other related systems
Described further in OMV1, FMS, Navigation section of this Study Guide

Secondary Attitude Air Data Reference Unit (SAARU)

Secondary source for everything ADIRU provides
Processes information from its own air data and inertial reference sources
Transmits pitch and roll information to standby attitude indicator
Does not provide navigation position data
Described further in OMV1, FMS & Navigation sections

Heading Data Selection

Heading Reference Switch selects either magnetic (NORM) or true heading

Selected heading displays on
    ♦ PFDs   ♦ FMCs
    ♦ NDs   ♦ AFDS
True is normally selected
    ♦ North of 82°N
    ♦ South of 82°S
    ♦ In vicinity of Magnetic poles—as depicted on charts
Inboard Display Selector
    PFD—Displays PFD on inboard display and blanks outer display
    NAV—Displays ND and inhibits DSP selections to inboard display
    MFD—Allows display of DSP-selected display
    EICAS—Displays EICAS
        Inhibits most DSP selections except limited FUEL, ENG and AIR displays
        Blanks upper center display

Air Data

Three static ports on left, **four** on right side of airplane
Left and right static information is paired through pneumatic tubing to each of L, C, and R air data modules
Air data modules convert static air pressure to digital output used by various systems
Center static ports also connected to
    ♦ Independent air data module <u>to provide static pressure to</u>
    ♦ Standby airspeed indicator <u>and</u>
    ♦ Standby altimeter
Pitot Probes
    R & C probes on right side of aircraft forward section
    L probe on left side of aircraft forward section
    Each probe provides air source for respective air data module
    Air data modules process dynamic pressure information to digital output for other systems' use
    Center probe also provides dynamic pressure to standby air data module

Angle of Attack (AOA)

Two vanes, one on each side of forward fuselage
ADIRU provides primary data source for
    PFD AOA indicators
    SAARU is backup source
    If primary source fails, secondary backup selection is automatic
AOA signal generation is independent from pitot static system
Damage to nosecone and/or disruption of airflow over AOA vanes renders information unreliable

Total Air Temperature (TAT)

Probe mounted on forward fuselage left side
Temperature sensed by probe is used by ADIRU and SAARU to compute total air temperature

Static Air Temperature (SAT)

SAT displayed on CDU—**PROG** page 2 comes from ADIRU
If ADIRU data is invalid, SAARU computed value is used

Anti-Ice of Air Data Components

Occurs automatically
All components in this section are heated at all times when either engine is running OMV2, ANTI-ICE-3

Primary Flight Displays

Integrated display of all flight parameters

Failure Flags displayed for system failures
Displayed information is removed
  If source fails *OR*
  No system source information is available
Normally displayed information is replaced by dashes
  No valid information is available
  May be due to out-of-range or malfunctioning nav aids

Airspeed Display

Tape and digital window
Mach displayed when mach is greater than 0.40
Airspeed trend vector indicates predicted airspeed in 10 seconds
Selected airspeed is displayed above tape

Vertical Speed

Displayed to right of altitude tape
Digital display appears when VV is greater than 400 fpm
Selected vertical speed bug appears in AFDS V/S mode

Altitude Display

Altitude tape on right side of PFD
Digital altitude readout in box on center of tape
If meters selected on EFIS panel
  Current altitude in meters shown above altitude window
  Altitude in feet remains
  Selected altitude is displayed at top of tape in meters
Selected altitude from MCP window is displayed above altitude tape
  Boxed when approaching altitude
  Selected altitude is also displayed on "bug" on altitude tape
  Does not reflect VNAV parameters which may inhibit climb or descent to MCP window altitude
  Note: *This can be very confusing when an altitude selected and displayed on the PFD has not become active*
    Key is bug position—if bug is aligned with current altitude, then selected altitude from MCP is not where the airplane is going until the pilot changes something
Landing altitude reference bar displayed on inner edge of altitude tape
  1000-500 feet above touchdown, tape is white
  500-0 feet above touchdown, tape is amber
QNH and QFE settings are available
  AA uses only QNH
  PFD Altitude tape background color green indicates someone has left the mode in QFE

Attitude Indication

Fairly intuitive—only selected information presented here
Small rectangle under bank pointer indicates slip and skid conditions
Pitch limit indication is displayed
  At low speeds with flaps up
  Any time flaps are down

Steering Indications

TCAS Resolution Advisory steering appears in attitude information area
Flight Path Vector (FPV) symbol
  Represents airplane flight path angle vertically *and*
    Airplane drive angle laterally
  Appears when EFIS FPV switch is on *or*
    MCP FPA reference switch is on
Flight Path Angle (FPA) symbol
  Shows selected flight path angle
  Appears when MCP FPA reference switch is on *and*
    Either FD or AP is engaged
Display of FPA and FPV is larger and brighter if FD is off

Radio Altitude

Displayed when radio altitude sensors detect airplane is less than 2,500 feet above source
Always on—will appear in cruise flight when another airplane passes less than 2,500 feet below

Angle of Attack Indication

Upper right corner of PFD
Digital and analog displays
Shows:
  Stick shaker point
  Zero reference line—4:30 position
  Additional reference lines every 5 degrees from -5 to +20
Data is computed—not raw data

Engine Fail, GPWS, and PWS Alerts

Displayed in large capital letters between attitude display and heading/track compass rose
  Refer to OMV1, Warning Systems section

Navigation Displays (ND)

Only selected information for review is presented. Most information is well covered in simulators and other training devices. Only easily forgotten and occasionally asked-for information is contained in these notes.

Position Trend Vector

Three dashed lines
Represent predicted position at 30, 60, and 90 seconds
  Based on bank angle and ground speed
  For ranges greater than 20 miles .... 3 segments
  For 20 NM range .... 2 segments
  For 10 NM range .... 1 segment
VNAV Path Pointer
Displays vertical deviation from VNAV computed path
Appears when airplane first gets within ±400' from path
Only appears in descent
Digital display appears when more than 400' from path

TCAS Indications

See Warning Systems notes, *page 56*

CDU L, C, R ND Source Indication

Indicated map source (Green)
Displays ND Source if
  CDU is selected on navigation source select switch *OR*
  Both FMCs fail *OR*
  A manually selected FMC fails

ILS Park Annunciation

Indicates ILS receivers are untuned
Displayed at power up until
  200NM from touchdown *OR*
  Halfway to destination, whichever occurs first
Remains in view until receivers are tuned

Acronyms

ADIRS	air data inertial reference system
ADIRU	air data inertial reference unit
ADM	air data modules
AIMS	airplane information management system
CDU	control display unit
DSP	display select panel
EFIS	electronic flight information system
FD	flight director
FPA	flight path angle
FPV	flight path vector
LNAV	lateral navigation
MFD	multi-function display
ND	navigation display
PFD	primary flight display
PWS	predictive wind shear
SAARU	secondary attitude air data reference unit
VNAV	vertical navigation

Flight Management, Navigation

This section contains only selected notes specific to the 777. Many aspects of navigation are common to other aircraft with which pilots are familiar.

Navigation System Inputs

- ◆ VOR
- ◆ DME
- ◆ ILS
- ◆ ADF
- ◆ Global Positioning System (GPS)
- ◆ Air Data Inertial Reference System (ADIRS)
- ◆ Flight Management System (FMS)
- ◆ ATC Transponder

Global Positioning System (GPS)

FMC Computes position
Uses inertial reference inputs continually
Uses GPS for position updates to fine-tune position

Annunciation on ND is GPS when FMC uses GPS inputs
Two independent GPS receivers
GPS tunes automatically

If ADIRU becomes inoperative
EICAS displays message **NAV ADIRU INERTIAL**
FMC uses only GPS data to navigate

GPS Inoperative
EICAS displays message **GPS**
Indicates both receivers
Inoperative *OR*
Unavailable

GPS updates allowed
For all United States National Airspace approach ops
Outside this region, allowed during approaches <u>only if</u>
FMC database and approach charts are referenced to WGS-84 reference datum
Other approaches not in above category
GPS should be inhibited for approaches *unless*
Other appropriate procedures are used
<u>Practical implication</u>: All approaches in issued manuals are be in A/C database and are legal to be flown using GPS

Inhibiting GPS data inputs
Can be accomplished with **GPS NAV PROMPT** on **POS REF** page of FMC (Page 3/3).............................See OMV1, APP/LANDING-6

Inertial System

Air Data Inertial Reference System (ADIRS)
Calculates flight parameters to include
- ◆ Position
- ◆ Speed
- ◆ Altitude
- ◆ Attitude

Provides this data to
- ◆ Displays
- ◆ Flight Controls
- ◆ Flight Management System
- ◆ Engine Controls

Major components are ADIRU and SAARU modules

Air Data Inertial Reference Unit (ADIRU)
Provides primary
Flight data
Inertial reference
Air data
Power
Initial power-up requires battery power, and ADIRU switch on
If ADIRU is turned off, full realignment required before aircraft is moved
ON BAT Light—illuminates when
- ◆ **ADIRU** is selected **ON** *and*
- ◆ Ground power or primary power subsequently is removed or fails
Hot battery bus continues to supply power
Ground crew call horn in nose gear well calls attention to ADIRU on battery power
When ADIRU is switched off
Ground—Remains powered for "a few seconds"
Flight—System logic prevents ADIRU from losing power

Alignment
Time to alignment complete is on ND upper left corner
Airplane should not move during alignment time
Position must be confirmed / entered
If entered position differs significantly from position of origin airport, scratchpad message
.............................**INERTIAL / ORIGIN DISAGREE**
If internal ADIRU comparison tests do not pass, scratchpad message.........................**ENTER INERTIAL POSITION**
If entered position fails comparison test twice, scratchpad message ....**ALIGNMENT REINITIATED**
If ADIRU position is "far different" from GPS position, EICAS message ....**NAV UNABLE RNP**
Automatic realignment mode—velocity and acceleration errors are reset to zero
No in-flight ADIRU realignment is possible
Position realignment recommended if total time in navigation mode exceeds 24 hours

Secondary Attitude and Air Data Reference Unit (SAARU)
Secondary data source of critical flight data for displays and other systems
If ADIRU fails
SAARU automatically supplies
- ◆ Attitude
- ◆ Heading
- ◆ Air data
In non-polar region, magnetic heading must be periodically updated
If ADIRU Inertial data fails
EICAS caution message **NAV ADIRU INERTIAL**
SAARU provides
Attitude data to PFDs
Three minutes of heading data in non-polar regions
Heading based on ADIRU heading prior to failure
Control Display Unit (CDU) prompt after three minutes: **SET HDG**
Heading must be "periodically updated" thereafter without further prompts
SAARU heading continues to be provided until aircraft decelerates below 100 knots
Numerous navigation modes and functions inoperative in this backup mode—see OMV2 for specifics
Some capabilities are restored after SAARU heading update
Autobrakes are inoperative
No **LNAV** or **VNAV** mode capability
SAARU is sole source of data to standby attitude indicator display
Power up
Completely automatic at airplane power-up
No SAARU controls available to crew

Air Data and Attitude Sources

Three Channel System
Left, center and right pitot and static systems
ADIRU and SAARU share data from these channels
Air data modules—remote sensors for air data functions
Both ADIRU and SAARU receive data from
All air data modules
Both AOA vanes
Dual element TAT probe
Air data is considered valid for ADIRU and SAARU when two or more channels agree
When ADIRU air data is invalid *and*
AIR DATA SOURCE switch is in **OFF** position,
Valid SAARU air data is used
Single channel operation
Occurs when ADIRU and SAARU data are invalid
Left PFD displays—**ADIRU** data from **L** pitot static system
Right PFD displays—**SAARU** data from **R** pitot static system
EICAS message **NAV AIR DATA SYS**
Left PFD receives data from L pitot static system
Standby Instruments
Receive data from center pitot-static ports *through*
Standby air data modules
Attitude and airspeed displays are independent of ADIRU and SAARU values

Radio Navigation Systems

Automatic Direction Finding (ADF)

Two systems
Either ADF may be manually tuned from either left or right CDU
ND data displays ADF when related VOR/ADF switch in **ADF** position
ADF data displays in CYAN
If both FMCs fail, L and R ADFs may be tuned on related L and R CDU **ALTN NAV RADIO** page

Distance Measuring Equipment (DME)

Two installed
Normally auto-tuned
FMC tunes DME as needed for radio position updates
Can be manually tuned on FMC nav radio page
> **Note:** *Manual DME tuning does not inhibit FMC DME tuning*
FMC uses two DMEs and triangulation to update position

Instrument Landing System (ILS)

Three receivers
Usually tuned automatically by FMC when
ILS, LOC back course, LDA or SDF approach selected for the active route
Runway is within
50 NM from the top of descent *OR*
150 NM of the landing runway threshold, *OR*
FMC is in **DESCENT** mode
Initial takeoff—ILS autotuning inhibited for 10 minutes to prevent PFD clutter
Selection and execution of an approach on active route during inhibited period overrides this limit
Inhibition does not apply on subsequent takeoffs on same flight (touch and go, etc.)
ILS Tuning Inhibit active when
AP is engaged and localizer or glideslope is captured *OR*
FD is engaged, and either localizer or glideslope is captured with airplane below 500' radio altitude *OR*
On ground, localizer is alive, airplane heading is within 45 degrees of localizer front course with airspeed greater than 40 knots
ILS Auto tuning is re-enabled when
Either **TO/GA** switch is pressed *OR*
The autopilot is disengaged and both FDs are switched off *OR*
MCP **APP** mode is deselected above 1500' radio altitude
Automatic retuning occurs when
ILS auto tuning is enabled *AND*
A new approach is selected on the CDU
After Dual FMC failure
L and C ILS receivers are tuned with the L CDU
R ILS receiver is tuned with R CDU
Accomplished on the CDU **ALTN NAV RADIO** page
Can be manually tuned

NAVAID Identifier Decoding

Morse coded identifiers of tuned signals are automatically converted to alpha characters
Decoded identifiers appear on PFD
Verifying identifier with approach procedure is adequate for identifying correct navaid
Audio tuning is required if identifier does not display correctly as expected
Decoding applies to VOR, ILS, DME, and ADF

VOR Receivers

Two installed
FMC can tune VOR and collocated DME for position updates
FMC uses VOR / DME radio updates when more accurate sources are not available
Manual tuning
Accomplished by entering identifier or frequency
Inhibits automatic tuning until manual station is deleted
After Dual FMC failure
L and R CDUs tune respective VOR receiver
ALT NAV RADIO page of CDU is used
ND displays of VOR
Normally FMCs both tune same VOR
VOR bearing information appears in map display when
EFIS **VOR/ADF** switch is in **VOR** *AND*
Either or both **VOR L** or **VOR R** switches are selected
VOR course deviation is displayed only in EFIS **VOR** mode

Transponder

Panel controls
Two ATC transponders
TCAS system
EICAS Advisory message
TRANSPONDER L or R
Indicates selected transponder failure
If altitude reporting fails, alternate source can be selected
Transponder information sources
NORM Altitude source selected—ADIRU
ALT Altitude source selected—SAARU
Therefore, **NORM** is always selected on preflight
See Warning Systems section, OMV2 for further information

Vertical Navigation

> **Note:** *VNAV is adequately taught except for occasional hot items. These are gradually being added to this Study Guide.*

On Approach

VNAV On Approach mode is a non-annunciated mode which is important to understand
When active, allows the following:
IAS/MACH window can be opened and the command speed set while VNAV remains in VNAV PTH descent
MCP Altitude can be set above A/C altitude for missed approach
VNAV remains in VNAV PTH and follows descent path unless:
♦ Airplane accelerates to within 5 knots of current flap placard *and*
♦ Airplane rises 150 feet above path
In this case, mode changes to VNAV SPD
Glide path angle, if specified on one or more legs of the approach procedure, is displayed when the mode becomes active
Becomes active when any of the following occur:
Airplane is in descent mode *and* flaps are out of UP
A VFR approach has been created and incorporated into the active flight plan *and*
♦ The airplane has sequenced the FAXXX fix *or*
♦ The airplane is enroute to a direct-to or intercept-to the RWXXX waypoint and the airplane is within 25NM of the runway threshold
A published instrument approach has been selected and incorporated into the active flight plan *and*
♦ The airplane has sequenced (passed) the first waypoint on the published approach *or*
♦ The airplane is enroute to a direct-to or intercept-to waypoint (1L on RTE page) and the airplane is within 12NM of the runway threshold *or*
♦ The airplane is enroute to a direct-to or intercept-to waypoint (1L on RTE page) *that is the last waypoint in the approach* (runway or missed approach point) and the airplane is within 25NM of *that waypoint*

Flight Management System (FMS)

Acronyms

ADIRS ....air data inertial reference system
ADIRU ....air data inertial reference unit
CDU ....control data unit
DSP ....Display selector panel
FMC...Flight management computer
FMS..flight management system
GPS ....global positioning system
MCP ....mode control panel
MFD ....Multifunction display
ND ....navigation display
PFD ....primary flight display
SAARU................secondary attitude and air data reference unit

Components

Flight management computer (FMC)
    Two independent computers
    Normally, one active, with the other backing it up and prepared to activate if failures occur
    Inputs
        Crew-entered flight plan data
        Airplane systems data
        FMC navigation database
    Outputs
        Calculated present position
        Pitch, roll, and thrust commands to fly optimal profile
        Commands sent to APs, ATs, and FDs
        Map and route data sent to NDs
    MCP used to select A/T, AP, and FD modes

Control Display Unit (CDU)
    Three mechanically identical units
    L and R are used for pilot navigation and some communication inputs
    C is used for communications and maintenance functions
        SATCOM, flight interphone selections
        Can be used to back up L and R CDU in event of failure
        Can be used to select alternate display controls
    300ER Brightness adjustment is a rocker switch

Fuel System

General

Provides pressurized fuel to engines and APU
Fuel contained in center, left and right wing tanks

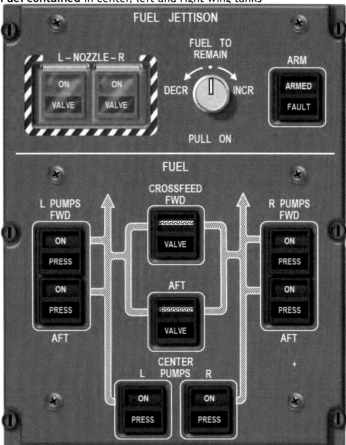

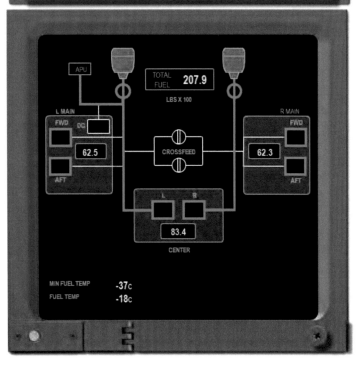

Fuel Measuring

Quantity
Sensors in each tank
Total fuel on primary EICAS display
Individual quantities displayed on fuel synoptic
Temperature
Displayed on primary EICAS display
Normally white; Amber when approaching minimum allowed
Minimum fuel temperature can be changed on FMS CDU
TO REMAIN amount replaces temperature display when dumping
Actual and min temperatures always displayed on fuel synoptic

Fuel Pumps

Two AC pumps in each tank
Any single pump has enough output to supply fuel to operate one engine under all conditions
Center tank pumps
Override/jettison pumps
Higher output pressure than wing tank pumps
Allows center tank fuel to be used before wing tank fuel
Low output pressure with more than 2400 lbs of fuel remaining **FUEL PUMP CENTER L** or **R** advisory message displays
Low output pressure with less than 2400 lbs of fuel remaining **FUEL LOW CENTER** EICAS advisory message displays
Scavenge system
Automatically to transfers remaining fuel from center tank
Process begins as wing tank quantity reduces (either L or R) to less than 29,000 lbs. **200ER** or 52,600 **300ER**
Center tank must be <35,000 lbs. (both **200ER** and **300ER**
Load shedding
On ground, only one center tank pump operates unless two AC sources are available
With only one AC power source
Only one pump operates
PRESS light on non-powered side is illuminated
Pump pressure EICAS message is inhibited
Indications with pump switches OFF
Main tank pumps—**PRESS** light in switch and EICAS message
Center tank pumps—Switch **PRESS** light and low pressure EICAS message inhibited

Left Main Tank DC Pump

Provides pressurized fuel to APU automatically when:
APU Selector is on and
No AC power is available
No controls for pump
Only indicator is on fuel synoptic
In flight operates automatically with loss of all AC to allow for:
Quick left engine relight following loss in flight
APU start
Also used on ground for battery start of left engine

Suction Feed

Can provide fuel to respective engine from main tanks
Designed to work if main tank pump output pressure is low
Suction feed lines bypass pumps
Dissolved air
Can cause air bubbles as pressure lowers in climb
Bubbles dissipate after stabilizing at cruise altitude
Depletion time depends on altitude, temperature & fuel type
Suction feed is capable of providing sufficient fuel to operate engines after dissolved air depletes

300ER Nitrogen Generation System

Converts bleed air to nitrogen-enriched air
Reduces flammability potential
Active during all phases of flight and for a brief period after landing
System is shut down when:
♦ Single engine operations *OR*
♦ Equipment cooling switch **OFF** *OR*
♦ Cargo Fire Arm switch is **ARMED**

Fuel Filters

Low Pressure Fuel Filter—between first and second stage of engine fuel pump

Pressure drop between filter inlet and outlet sets **ENG FUEL FILTER** (**L** or **R**) status message

Single channel indication system—so message can mean indication failure

If the filter subsequently is blocked, a bypass line allows fuel to continue flowing to secondary pump ...QRH ENG, APU 7.26

High Pressure Fuel Filter—Strainer downstream of second stage pump, fuel metering and flow meter

Prevents blockages at engine combustor fuel spray nozzles

No bypass or indication system

Note: *High pressure fuel filter information removed from OM*

Crossfeed

Allows pressurized fuel from one main tank to feed both engines

Prolonged operation causes progressively larger fuel imbalance

Can also be used to balance fuel in main tanks

Crossfeed manifolds arranged so any pump can supply both engines (may not be sufficient for max fuel flow in all conditions)

Crossfeed valves closed in normal operations

Tanks then operate in isolation with one center pump and main tank pumps providing fuel to respective engine

Valve position disagreement with valve results in

Crossfeed switch **VALVE** light *AND*

EICAS advisory message **FUEL CROSSFEED FWD** or **AFT**

Fuel Imbalance

If **quantity disagrees** between left and right main tanks by an "excessive quantity"

EICAS advisory message **FUEL IMBALANCE**

Balance attained through crossfeed

Amount required to turn message on varies with total main tank fuel quantity

See LIMITATIONS for allowable imbalance (or *page 11* of this study guide)

Imbalance pointer appears if main tank fuel differs L to R by more than 1000 pounds

If a crossfeed valve is open, pointer appears if difference is over 200 pounds

If message **FUEL IMBALANCE** is present, triangle becomes amber and is filled rather than empty white triangle

Imbalance pointer flashes if balance is getting larger rather than smaller

When fuel back in balance, **FUEL BALANCED** replaces **FUEL QTY** on expanded display for 5 seconds and flashes

Fuel Tank Capacities

Nominal values	Gallons	Pounds
Left or Right Main	9,560	64,000
Center	26,100	174,900
Total	45,200	302,900

300ER Nominal values	Gallons	Pounds
Left or Right Main	10,300	69,000
Center	27,290	182,800
Total	47,890	320,800

For variations due to density, see LIMITATIONS of OMV1, or *page 11* of this study guide

Synoptic Fuel Spar Anomaly

L AC bus power interruption can cause invalid spar valve display

When this occurs, fuel synoptic should not be used for situational awareness.

Synoptic page on the CA inboard, FO inboard and lower MFD may show different indications

Indications:

Fuel Synoptic page shows fuel spar valve as invalid (gray circle)

Green fuel flow bars replaced with white background

APU Fuel Feed

Fuel supplied from left fuel manifold

Sources

Any main or center tank pump which is pressurizing left fuel manifold

DC pump in left main tank if no AC power is available to power another pump

With AC power available and all boost pump switches **OFF**

Left forward pump operates automatically *AND*

DC pump turns off

In flight with loss of all AC power, DC pump turns on automatically

Allows for quick left engine relight

Also allows for start of APU with no AC power

Jettison System

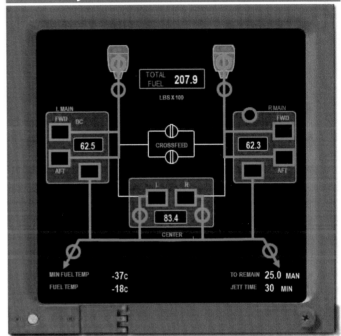

Jettison begins when:

Fuel tank jettison **ARMED** switch is **ON** *AND*

Fuel nozzle switches are **ON** *AND*

Jettison nozzle valves are **OPEN** *AND*

Main tank jettison pumps operate

Jettison terminates when:

Fuel quantity total reaches the value set in the fuel to remain display *OR*

Fuel jettison nozzles are both closed *OR*

Fuel jettison arm switch is disarmed *OR*

A fault is sensed in the jettison system *OR*

Fuel quantity in each main tank decreases to **200ER** 11,500 lbs. / **300ER** 8,500 lbs. *OR*

Aircraft is on the ground

Jettison Sequencing

All tanks jettison simultaneously unless CG stability requires Center tank to be delayed in dumping

Fuel synoptic is modified to show dump status, including valves and pumps

Jettison Progress

Fuel Synoptic displays pump status and fuel flow to wing nozzles

Expanded fuel EICAS display shows both time remaining and the amount of fuel scheduled to remain when dump is completed

When parameters above are reached, jettison terminates

Dump Rates

Fuel in center tank (as well as wing tanks) ....5,400 PPM

Fuel only remaining in wing tanks ....3,100 PPM

QRH Fuel 12.2

Hydraulics

General Features

Three independent systems—Left, right, center

Used to control
- ◆ Flight controls
- ◆ Leading edge slats
- ◆ Trailing edge flaps
- ◆ Landing gear
- ◆ Wheel brakes
- ◆ Nose and main gear steering
- ◆ Thrust reversers

Flight controls distributed among three systems
   Any one system provides adequate aircraft control
Reservoirs for each system pressurized by bleed air

Left & Right Systems

Each system powers
- ◆ Flight control components
- ◆ Respective thrust reverser

  <u>Difference</u>—Right system powers normal brakes as well
Primary pumps—Mechanically driven
  One on each engine
Demand pumps
  Electrically-powered
  Supplementary pressure for high-demand situations
  Backup for primary pump failure
  Auto position—pumps run when:
    Takeoff & landing (flaps extended)
    System or primary pump pressure drops
    On ground—right pump operates continuously

Center System

Key components powered

- ◆ Flight controls
- ◆ Alternate brakes
- ◆ Reserve brakes *
- ◆ Landing Gear actuation
- ◆ Leading Edge Slats
- ◆ Trailing Edge Flaps
- ◆ Main gear steering
- ◆ Nose gear steering

***Note**: *Removed from Landing Gear description of brake system, but still appears in Hydraulic System section of OMV2*
Ram Air Turbine (**RAT**)—Backup pressure for primary flight controls only

Primary Pumps

Two electrically powered pumps
Designated C1 and C2 pumps
Load shedding
  <u>Ground</u> with only one AC source
    ◆ C1 pump runs at all times when selected
    ◆ C2 pump does not run if C1 is running
    With two AC sources (including primary and secondary external AC) both pumps run
  <u>In flight</u> C2 may load shed by ELMS in following conditions:
    ◆ All other electrical pumps are running **OR**
    ◆ Only one AC source is available **OR**
    ◆ Generator capacity is exceeded
  When conditions for load shedding no longer exist, pumps are powered again automatically

Demand Pumps

Air driven
Supplementary pressure for high demand
Backup for primary pump failures
Controlled by C1 and C2 demand pump selectors
AUTO position—pumps run if:
  ◆ System and/or primary pump pressure low **OR**
  ◆ System logic anticipates high demand
ON position—pump(s) run continuously
  Both pump selectors **ON**—only C1 operates
  Both pumps cannot run simultaneously
Demand Pump Fault Lights display for
  ◆ Low demand pump output pressure
  ◆ Excessive demand pump fluid pressure
  ◆ Demand pump is selected **OFF**

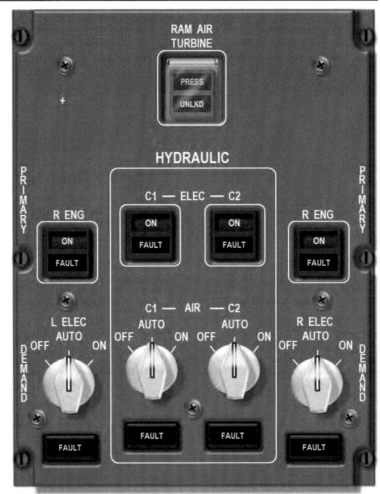

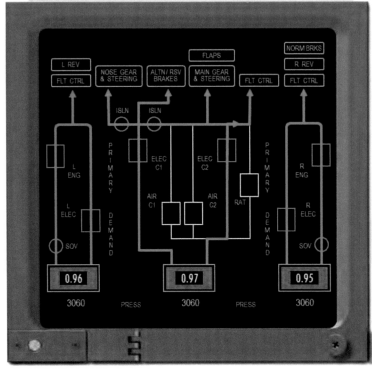

Synoptic Indications

Quantity—reservoir volume as a percentage of normal service level (1.00 is the normal service level) .... `0.95`
Reservoir quantity low .... `0.15 LO`
Quantity over full (inhibited in flight).................... `1.05 OF`
Quantity requires refilling (Inhibited in flight) .... `.72 RF`
Pressure of highest output pump pressurizing system
.... `PRESS 3010`

Synoptic graphic symbols

Pressurized line... —

Unpressurized line .... —

Flow direction .... ←

Hydraulic valve not in commanded position .... ⊗

Valve with invalid sensor data .... ⊘

Pump commanded on with pressure low .... ⊠

Pump commanded on with normal pressure .... ⊟

Pump with invalid data from sensor .... ▭

Center Non-Normal Operation

Leak isolation logic protects key systems
If a leak is detected
  Two branches isolated from center system pressure
    Nose gear actuation / steering
    Leading edge slats
  One branch isolated and pressurized by C1 pump—**ALTN/RSV**
    BRAKES
  Remainder of center system
  Isolated and pressurized by C2 pump
  C1 and C2 demand pumps operate if required
Reservoir fluid quantity drop detected
  Flap/slat electronic Units prevent slats from operating in
    primary (hydraulic) mode
  Prevents slat retraction if loss due to catastrophic engine
    failure in critical phase of flight
  LE slats are reconnected to center system and operate in the
    normal mode If:
    System volume recovers to normal for 5 seconds **AND**
    System detects both engines running more than 30 seconds
Reserve isolation valve remains closed for remainder of flight
to isolate
  ♦ Main landing gear actuation & steering
  ♦ Flap & slat operation
  ♦ Center system flight controls
Nose gear isolation valve opens to restore pressure to nose
gear actuation and steering if:
  ♦ Center system flight control pressure _drops_
    Leak is assumed to be in main landing gear, flaps or flight
      control lines
    Nose gear isolation valve opens and C1 primary pump
      pressurizes nose gear branch
    In this case, ALTN/RSV BRAKES branch remains pressurized
  _OR_
  ♦ Center system flight control pressure _is maintained_
    Lowering gear handle opens **W** branch valve if both engines
      running and both primary engine-driven pumps are
      providing pressure
    Ensures primary pump pressure is available for both left
      and right system flight controls and normal brakes
      before opening valve
    Nose gear branch leak in this situation could cause loss of
      center system
  _OR_
  ♦ Single engine operation
    Above conditions would not be met
    NG branch valve opens when AC slows below 60 knots
    Allows steering when rudder effectiveness is lost

Ram Air Turbine

Priority Output

Provides hydraulic power to center system primary flight
  controls
Provides electrical power
  Power for standby system switches to Battery if RAT sheds
    electrical power generation
  See Electrical notes, _page 32_ of this Study Guide for electrical
    functions of RAT.
Priority is hydraulic pressure over electrical power generation

Deployment

Deploys if: (HEED)
  Hydraulic—All 3 hydraulic system pressures are low **OR**
  Electrical—Both AC transfer busses are unpowered **OR**
  Engines both fail **AND** center hydraulic pressure low **OR**
  Deployed manually

Manual deployment by pressing ram air turbine switch
  Hot battery or APU Battery bus must be powered
  Center hydraulic system does not need to be pressurized
  Deployment is by compressed spring
  RAT cannot be stowed in flight once deployed
Ram Air Turbine Switch
  Pressing the switch deploys the RAT if not
    already deployed
  PRESS—RAT is deployed _and_
    Center primary flight control hydraulic
      pressure is greater than 1500 psi
  UNLKD—RAT is _not_ in the stowed position

Landing Gear

Key Components

Steering
Nosewheel
Aft pair on each main gear truck
Braking
Main gear wheels only
Normal brake pressure from right hydraulic system
Alternate brakes on center hydraulic system
Antiskid provided with all braking modes
Autobrakes only available with normal brakes
Monitoring on GEAR synoptic
Tire pressure readouts for each wheel
Brake temperature monitors on each brake

Air/Ground sensing system

In-flight and ground operation of many systems changes depending on air or ground mode of airplane
Sensors located on each main landing gear beam

Landing Gear Operation

Gear Lever
Automatic lever lock secures handle down on ground
In-flight lever lock is automatically retracted through air-ground sensors
Manual override possible by pressing and holding the landing gear lever lock override switch
Retraction
Sequence
Gear handle moved to up
Gear begins to retract
EICAS gear green **DOWN** indication changes to white crosshatch transition indication
Main gear doors open
Main gear wheels tilt to retract position
When retraction complete, indication changes to green **UP** indication
After 10 seconds, indication disappears
Abnormal retraction
After normal time allowance for retraction, if retraction not complete—EICAS **GEAR DISAGREE** caution message displayed
Indication changes to expanded non-normal format
Affected gear displayed as in-transit down
Occurs if the gear is not unlocked from down position in normal time allotment
EICAS **GEAR DOOR** advisory message is displayed
Note: *WOW system can delay ground-air transition (as long as 17 seconds) if TO weight is light (<490K lbs) and 2 preceding landing weights were heavy (>525K lbs). This information removed from OM.*
Extension
Sequence
Gear handle moved to down
Main gear doors open
EICAS gear in transition crosshatch appears
Gear free-falls without hydraulic pressure
Downlocks are powered to the locked position

Hydraulically operated gear doors close
Main gear trucks tilt to flight position
When gear are locked down, EICAS gear indication changes to **DOWN**
Down indication means:
Side and drag brace on each main gear is in down and locked position *and*
Nose gear drag brace is in down and locked position
Extension Abnormalities
After normal time allowance for extension, if any gear is not locked down—EICAS **GEAR DISAGREE** caution message displayed *and*
Audible beeper warning sounds
If gear does not lock down in expected time
Indication changes to expanded non-normal format
Affected gear displayed as in-transit down *or*
UP indication if respective gear never unlocked
If gear doors do not reclose in expected transit time, EICAS **GEAR DOOR** message is displayed
If only one brace on a main gear is locked
EICAS caution message **MAIN GEAR BRACE L** or **R** *and* audible beeper warning sounds
EICAS gear position indicator shows expanded non-normal display

Landing Gear Alternate Extension

Dedicated DC electrically powered hydraulic pump
Uses center hydraulic system fluid
Releases the uplocks on gear doors and landing gear
Gear allowed to free-fall into position
Landing gear lever has no effect on system
EICAS
Displays expanded gear position indication when using this system
GEAR DOOR message is displayed because doors remain open
After alternate extension
Landing gear may be retracted if the normal system is operating
Select **DN** then **UP** on gear handle to retract

Nose Wheel and Main Gear Aft Axle Steering

Nose wheel steering tiller
Allows nose wheel steering up to **70°**
Powered by center system
A pointer on the tiller shows the relative position
Rudder pedal steering—can steer nose wheel up to **7°**
Main Gear Aft Axle Steering
Begins when nose wheel steering angle exceeds **13°**
Reduces tire scrubbing
Takeoff configuration warning message
CONFIG GEAR STEERING
Part of the takeoff configuration warning system
Indicates the main gear have not returned to a straight alignment when commanded to the center position when takeoff thrust is selected

Brake System

Main Gear Brake Features

Each wheel has a multiple carbon-disc brake set
Nose wheels have no brakes
Wear Indicator pins on each wheel must protrude beyond flush with parking brakes set

Normal Brakes

Right hydraulic system provides fluid to power brakes
Each brake pedal controls respective L and R wheel brakes

Alternate Brakes

Selection is automatic
If right system pressure is low
Center / reserve system automatically supplies pressure
Pressing a brake pedal sends hydraulic pressure through alternate antiskid valves to brakes
If center system quantity is low
C1 primary pump is isolated from center hydraulic system
Provides an alternate braking pressure source
Both right and center systems have low pressure
BRAKE SOURCE light illuminates

EICAS advisory message **BRAKE SOURCE**
Normal and alternate brake system
pressures are low, **AND**
Reserve hydraulic source for alternate brake
system is low

EICAS advisory message **RESERVE BRAKE / STRG**
The following may not be available:
- ♦ Alternate brakes from the reserve hydraulic source **OR**
- ♦ Normal nose gear extension **OR**
- ♦ Nose wheel steering

Brake Accumulator

Located in normal brake hydraulic system
Pressure is recharged by right system
Pressure is indicated on brake accumulator pressure indicator
below captain's PFD
If right and **center / reserve hydraulic** systems are lost
Brake accumulator is available with no switch actions
Can provide several applications **or**
Parking brake application

Anti-Skid

Works in all brake modes
Normal mode—Wheels independently controlled
Alternate brakes—Brakes controlled as follows:
Forward and center on each side of each
truck paired
Aft truck wheels independently controlled
Control Information
Touchdown and hydroplaning protection uses
inertial ground speed values
Locked wheel protection compares wheel
speed to other wheels
EICAS **ANTISKID** message indicates one of the
following:
Antiskid fault detected on brake system in use
Parking valve not fully open with parking brake
released
System is completely inoperative

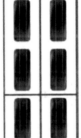

Autobrake System

Available only with normal brake system
Antiskid is provided with autobrakes
Selectable positions for landing
Armed by selecting prior to landing

Activated—braking application begins when
Both thrust levers are retracted to idle **and**
The wheels have spun up

Selectable levels
AUTOBRAKE 1 through **4**
AUTOBRAKE MAX
AUTOBRAKE RTO (rejected takeoff)—
takeoff position
Arming--Selecting prior to takeoff
arms the system
Activating—RTO autobrake selects
maximum braking pressure
if:
Airplane is on the ground **and**
Groundspeed is > 85 knots **and**
Both thrust levers are retarded to idle
Maximum braking is obtained in this mode
If takeoff is rejected below 85 knots groundspeed,
autobrakes do not activate

Autobrakes, if operative, must be armed prior to landing
when any of the following exist:
- ♦ Runway:
Short: Runway length less than 7000 feet
Slippery: Braking conditions reported less than
good
Contaminated: Runway contaminated with standing
water, snow, slush, or ice
- ♦ Weather RVR less than 4000 or visibility less than 3/4
mile (Minimum setting—3)
- ♦ Approach speed increased above normal by procedure.
Autobrakes are recommended when landing with **gusty
winds or crosswinds**
See OMV1, APPROACH-LANDING-G/A – 15.1,
25.9, 35.3, 40.5, 40.7

Autobrake application is metered
Achieves programmed deceleration rates
As other deceleration means take effect, autobraking
decreases to achieve targeted rates

For awareness only—according to instructor presentation:
Autobrake levels correspond to target deceleration rates
in feet per second as follows:
Autobrake 1................................4 FPS deceleration
Autobrake 2................................5 FPS deceleration
Autobrake 3................................6 FPS deceleration
Autobrake 4................................7 FPS deceleration
Autobrake Max..........................11 FPS deceleration
Autobrake RTO ....Maximum possible deceleration
Note: *Any abort over 80 knots using maximum braking (RTO)*
requires maintenance inspection prior to subsequent takeoff
...QRH LDG GEAR 14.5
Use in normal conditions—"For normal landing conditions,
autobrakes 2 or 3 will optimize brake wear, passenger comfort
and stopping performance." ....OMV1, Systems 80.5
Taxi brake release
Feature active when taxi speed less than 45 knots
Antiskid releases one axle pair of main gear brakes during
each brake application
Axle pair is sequentially changed on each application
Extends brake life and reduces brake sensitivity
Feature is NOT active for any of the following:
Any brake system except normal is in use
"Heavy brake application" occurs (not defined)
Landing rollout
Rejected takeoff
Parking brake applied
AUTOBRAKE **Advisory message**—indicates Autobrake disarmed or
inoperative
Braking during landing
Five levels of deceleration available
1 through **4**, and **MAX**—see above
On dry runway, full pedal braking applies more
deceleration than any autobrake *landing* mode
AUTOBRAKE MAX
Results in **AUTOBRAKE LEVEL 4** until pitch angle <1°
Then **MAX AUTO** level braking commences
Deceleration level can be changed without disarming
system by rotating selector
To maintain selected deceleration rate, brake pressure is
varied as other deceleration forces are applied (reverse
thrust, spoilers, etc.)
Deactivation—Autobraking stops when any of the following occur:
- ♦ Full stop is attained (autobrake mode remains engaged)
- ♦ Pedal brakes are applied
- ♦ Either thrust lever is advanced after landing
- ♦ Speedbrake handle is moved to the **DOWN** detent after
speedbrakes have deployed on the ground
- ♦ **DISARM** or **OFF** is selected on the autobrake selector
- ♦ Autobrake fault
- ♦ Normal antiskid system fault
- ♦ Loss of inertial data from ADIRU
- ♦ Autobrakes are applied after loss of normal brake hydraulic
pressure
When disarmed after landing
Selector moves to **DISARM** position
Power is removed from the autobrake system
When disarmed after takeoff
Selector remains in **RTO**
Automatically moves to **OFF** after takeoff

Parking Brake

Can be set with either normal or alternate system pressurized
If neither normal nor alternate are available, parking brake
pressure is maintained by brake accumulator
When set, EICAS memo message **PARKING BRAKE SET**
If set when either engine is advanced to takeoff thrust
Takeoff configuration warning message **CONFIG PARKING BRAKE**
Aural alert sounds

Brake Temperature Indication

Digital values rate heat on each brake from 0 to 9.9 scale
Normal temperature range is 0.0-4.9
Empty white box for temperature range 0-2.9
Filled white box
Shown when any wheel's temperature is in the high end (3.0 –
4.9) of the normal range
Highest temperature wheel on each truck is shown with filled
box
Filled amber box
"High range" value, 5.0 – 9.9
EICAS advisory message **BRAKE TEMP** for values of 5.0 and
higher

Automatic Relay Summary for Takeoff & Landing

	Takeoff	Aborted Takeoff	Landing	Go-Around
Auto Brakes Arming & Activation	Armed in **RTO** position	Activated when: ♦ Airplane is on the <u>ground</u> **and** ♦ Groundspeed is > <u>85 knots</u> **and** ♦ Both thrust levers are retarded to <u>idle</u>	**Brakes applied when:** ♦ Both thrust levers are retracted to <u>idle</u> **and** ♦ The wheels have spun up	Brakes released when either thrust lever is advanced *(See below)*
Disarming & Deactivation		♦Full stop is attained (autobrake mode remains engaged) ♦Pedal brakes are applied ♦Either thrust lever is advanced after landing ♦Speedbrake handle is moved to the **DOWN** detent after speedbrakes have deployed on the ground ♦**DISARM** or **OFF** is selected on the autobrake selector ♦Autobrake fault ♦Normal antiskid system fault ♦Loss of inertial data from ADIRU ♦Autobrakes are applied after loss of normal brake hydraulic pressure		
Auto Spoiler	No arming	Either thrust reverser selected deploys ground spoilers	<u>Armed</u> when handle placed in ARMED position inflight <u>Activated</u> when: ♦ Gear on ground (not tilted) **AND** ♦ Thrust Levers both IDLE **OR** ♦ Either thrust lever moved to reverse idle detent	Retracted when either thrust lever is advanced to **TAKEOFF** range Handle moves to down/unarmed position

EICAS Display—Brakes & Tire Pressures

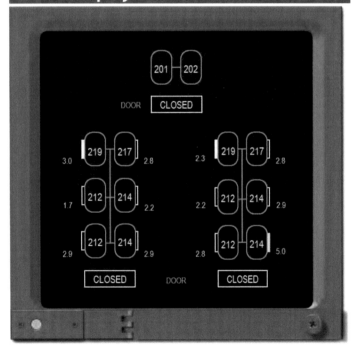

Tire Pressure Indication

Individual tire pressures displayed on gear synoptic
Allowable range is 0-400 psi
EICAS advisory message `TIRE PRESS`
 Indicates any tire is above or below normal range
 Also indicates excessive difference between two tires on same axle

`300ER` Tail Skid

Extends / retracts when landing gear handle is lowered / raised
EICAS Advisory `TAIL SKID` displayed when not in the correct position

Fault Indications

`BRAKE`—brake deactivation on associated wheel
`ASKID`—antiskid fault on associated wheel
Both appear on gear synoptic next to appropriate wheel

Warning Systems

Engine Indication and Crew Alerting System (EICAS)

General Features

Consolidates engine and airplane system indications
Primary display for system alerts and indications
Normally displayed on upper center display
Primary engine indications are also on upper center display

Master Warning and Caution Reset Switches & Lights

Press—Extinguishes Master Warning and/or
Master Caution light(s)
Silences aural tones associated with these
EICAS warning messages:

- ♦ **CABIN ALTITUDE**   ♦ **FIRE**
- ♦ **OVERSPEED** (some A/C)   ♦ **STABILIZER**
- ♦ **CONFIG GEAR**, if displayed because landing gear not down and locked, any thrust lever at idle, and radio altitude < 800 feet

Relights for each new Warning / Caution as they are initiated

EICAS Event Record Switch

Records up to five EICAS events into memory
When button pressed, records
Currently displayed engine indications
AND
Additional EICAS maintenance information
Without button pressed, if a system parameter is exceeded, automatically records out of limit parameters and related conditions
Located on forward aisle stand

EICAS Messages

Alert messages—crew alerting for non-normal conditions
From engine start to shutdown—primary means of crew alert
EICAS checklist steps contained in QRH
Rectangle ☐ appears left of the message if:
An alert has a checklist associated OR
No checklist, but notes or information of which crew needs to be aware

Alert Message Priority Levels

Warning .... ☐ RED
Cannot be cancelled
Accompanied by *aural bell* for fire warnings
Accompanied by *siren* for warnings of:
◆ Autopilot disconnect
◆ Cabin altitude
◆ Overspeed (some airplanes)
◆ Takeoff configuration warnings
Voice warnings for some other conditions
Preceded by a box ☐ indicating checklist steps exist if not completed or superseded by another procedure

Caution Message .... AMBER
New caution accompanied by *beeper* except for
ENGINE SHUTDOWN L or **R**
May be cancelled by pressing **CANC/ RCL** switch
May also be recalled by pressing the switch again
Note: *References to the* **CANC/RCL** *button in this section are for the display select panel button. Do not confuse with the* **CANC** *button on the ACARS message management button set.*

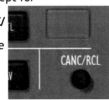

Advisory Message

Advisory Message .... AMBER
Next highest alert message
Indented one space from Warning and Caution messages
May be cancelled or recalled by pressing **CANC/RCL**

Communication messages .... ● WHITE
Preceded by white dot ◖ and indented one space
Cannot be cancelled or recalled by pressing **CANC/RCL**
Three priority levels—all are white in color
High—*Chime* associated with alert
Medium—*High-low chime* for new message
Low—No chime associated
All communication messages require crew action
Usually involves selecting Comm to display messages
Accomplishing action required makes message go away
Message cannot be cancelled other than by required action
If several COMM messages, most recent at *top* of list

Memo Messages .... WHITE
Status of selected flight-crew activated normal conditions
Appear at bottom of last page of EICAS alert messages
Pressing **CANC/RCL** button when last page of EICAS alert messages is displayed—ensures all current memos have been displayed
If several memo messages, most recent is at *bottom* of list

Status messages .... CYAN
A/C equipment faults
Faults so displayed are those affecting airplane dispatch
Displayed on MFD **STATUS** page
STATUS cue displays on primary EICAS display when new message appears
If several status messages, most recent is at *top* of list
STAT button
Displays single and multiple pages of status messages
Functions for status messages similarly to **CANC/RCL** button for EICAS messages

Display and Manipulation of Messages

Grouped by priority
WARNING messages (red) at top of list
CAUTION messages (amber) below last warning message
ADVISORY messages Indented one character to further demonstrate lower priority
Within groupings, most recently appearing message is at top of list
If a condition indicated by a message no longer exists
Message goes away AND
Items below move up one line to fill in

If more messages exist than can be displayed
Multiple pages are created
Pages are numbered, with numbers at bottom of list
If multiple pages of Caution and Advisory messages
Pages can be advanced with **CANC/RCL** button
If more Warning conditions exist than can be displayed
No page number shown
Pages *cannot* be advanced with **CANC/RCL** button
No other pages can be displayed
When at last page of caution and advisory messages
Pressing **CANC/RCL** button makes last of messages disappear and page go blank
Pressing again brings back first page of messages

Airspeed Alerts

Stall warning

Stick shakers used to alert crew to condition
Independent shakers on each control column

Airspeed low

Occurs when speed below min maneuvering
EICAS Caution **AIRSPEED LOW**
Amber box appears around current speed

Takeoff V1 Airspeed

VEE ONE sounds on takeoff when
Speed reaches V_1

Overspeed Warning

Occurs when speed is greater than V_{MO}/M_{MO}
EICAS message `OVERSPEED` is displayed
Message remains until condition goes away

Tail Strike Detection System

Detects ground contact that could damage airplane pressure hull
Sensors
  Two proximity sensors
  Two-inch blade antenna
  Installed on aft body of airplane
If detected, EICAS caution message, **TAIL STRIKE**
Tail strike protection through flight controls
Note: *For other flight envelope protection details see FLT-C section, page 39 of this book*

Takeoff & Landing Configuration Warnings
Takeoff Configuration Warning

EICAS Warning message `CONFIG` is displayed if the following are **all** met:
  ♦ **Ground**—Airplane is on the ground
  ♦ **Run**—Fuel control switches are in Run
  ♦ **Thrust**—Either engine thrust is in takeoff range
  ♦ **Speed**—Airspeed is less than V1
  AND Any one of the following configurations exist:
  ♦ **Doors** (any) not closed, latched and locked
  ♦ **Flaps** not in takeoff position
  ♦ **Main gear steering** not locked
  ♦ **Parking brake** set
  ♦ **Rudder trim** not centered
  ♦ **Speedbrake** handle not down
  ♦ **Stabilizer trim** not in green band
Inhibited at V_1
When message displays
  Siren sounds and master **WARNING** lights comes on
  Pressing **WARNING / CAUTION RESET** switch
    Resets the master warning lights
    Does not silence siren
  Siren remains on until
    Condition no longer exists *OR*
    Thrust Levers are retarded below takeoff range
  CONFIG message remains on 10 seconds after thrust levers retarded below takeoff range
    Aids in determining cause of siren

Landing Configuration Warning

Alerts the crew if the landing gear is not extended for landing
EICAS Warning message `CONFIG GEAR` is displayed if the following are **all** met:
  ♦ Airplane is in flight
  ♦ Any landing gear is not down and locked
  AND Either one of the following configurations exist:
  ♦ Radio altitude is less than 800 feet and either thrust lever is closed
  ♦ Flap handle is in landing position
If message is displayed because thrust lever is retarded at low altitude
  Pressing either master `WARNING` / `CAUTION` reset switch
    Silences siren
    Extinguishes master `WARNING` lights
  Message remains displayed until
    Thrust Levers advanced *OR*
    Landing gear is down and locked
If message is displayed because flap handle is in landing position without gear down and locked
  Siren cannot be silenced until
    Gear down and locked *OR*
    GND PROX GEAR OVRD switch is pressed
Message remains displayed as long as condition exists

Non-Normal Operation of Configuration Warning System

If system fails, EICAS advisory `CONFIG WARN SYS` message displayed
If TO and landing configuration system fails, **CONFIG** messages may or may not be displayed
If messages appear along with the `CONFIG WARN SYS` messages, the **CONFIG** messages may not be correct

MCP Selected Altitude Alerts

Purpose—Notify crew when approaching or departing altitude selected in MCP altitude window
Approaching MCP-selected altitude
  900' Before reaching selected altitude—white box appears around selected altitude and current altitude on PFD
  200' Before selected altitude—white boxes go away
Departing MCP selected altitude by 200 feet
  EICAS alert message `ALTITUDE ALERT`
  Amber box appears around current altitude
  Message and amber box disappear when:
    Altitude returns to within 200 feet of selected altitude *OR*
    New MCP altitude is selected *OR*
    Altitude continues to increase to more than 900 feet from MCP altitude selection
Altitude alert inhibits occur when
  Glideslope captured *OR*
  Landing flaps selected and landing gear down and locked

Traffic Alert & Collision Avoidance System (TCAS)
Controlled through Transponder Panel

TCAS Operating Policy

Both CA & FO must be qualified to operate
Visual contact made with traffic--See & Avoid
TCAS RA Issued—
  MUST comply with warning, even if traffic in sight
  Assures mutual collision avoidance actions occur, as coordinated through TCAS
Only vertical avoidance maneuvers are permitted in response to an RA
  If in a turn , continue the turn
  If "*INCREASE CLIMB*" RA occurs in a turn, level wings and climb at faster rate
Pilot Flying makes smooth, controlled responses
Assumed reaction time:
  5 Seconds from RA command issuance
  2.5 Seconds from reversal command for existing RA
No Enforcement action is to be taken against flight crews complying with TCAS who deviate from ATC clearance

Altitude Band Selection

ABOVE (ABV)—Used in Climb
  Traffic -2700 to +7000 from present altitude
Normal (N)—Used in cruise
  Traffic +2700' from present altitude
Below (BLW)—Used in Descent
  Traffic +2700 to -7000' from present altitude

Traffic Symbols and Warnings

Other Traffic ....Open White Diamond
  More than 6 miles away *OR*
  Over 1200' altitude differential
Proximate Traffic ....Filled White Diamond
  Within 6 Miles *AND*
  Within ± 1200' altitude
Traffic Advisory (TA) Intruder ......Filled Amber Circle
  Predicted path of another airplane which will enter TCAS conflict airspace within 25-45 seconds
    Aural Warning ....*TRAFFIC TRAFFIC*"
Resolution Advisory ....Filled Red Square
  Predicted path of another airplane which will enter TCAS conflict airspace within 20-30 seconds
  Threat is 25 seconds from closest point of approach
  Vertical avoidance maneuver displayed on IVSI
  If range farther than current ND scale, **OFFSCALE** displays on ND
    OMV2, 10.40.21 and 15.10.7 to 15.10.9
    Aural Warnings OMV2 15.20.6-to 15.20.8

Required flight crew response
Within 5 seconds of initial RA
Applying G-forces of ±.25 G
This is more than AP can supply, so response must be hand-flown (*no change from previous TCAS policy*)

Ground Proximity Warning System (GPWS)

GPWS Functions

Alerts crew of predicted ground proximity problems in any of six modes:
Mode 1—Excessive descent rate below 2450' AGL
Mode 2—Excessive terrain closure rate below 2450' AGL
See also modes 2A and 2B
Mode 3—Altitude loss after takeoff or go-around between 30 and 1330' AGL
Mode 4—Unsafe terrain clearance while not in landing configuration (either mode 4a or 4b)
Mode 5—Below glide slope more than 1.3 dots while below 1000' AGL
Windshear Mode—Significant windshear < 1500' AGL

Inhibit Switches

G/S Inhibit Switch
Pressed—Inhibits **BELOW GLIDE SLOPE** alerts when pressed below 1000' RA
GND PROX—Indicates GPWS alert occurring
Ground Proximity Gear Configuration Override Switch
Pressed—(**OVRD**—Amber)
Inhibits alerts for
TOO LOW GEAR
CONFIG GEAR
Ground Proximity Flap Override Switch
Pressed—(**OVRD**—Amber)
Inhibits **TOO LOW FLAPS** alert
Ground Proximity Terrain Override Switch
Pressed—(**OVRD**—Amber)
Inhibits look-ahead terrain alerts and display

Enhanced GPWS (EGPWS)

Major features
Worldwide database with all runways over 3500' long
(Not all of these can be displayed in map mode)
Terrain data from worldwide database can be shown
Warning capability if airplane flight path predicted to intersect terrain within specified criteria
Display
Variable density dot patterns
Dot density indicates height in respective color zone
ND TERR message annunciated when active

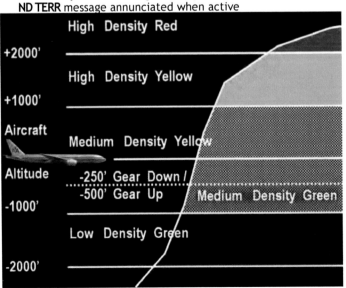

Alerts
Caution Alert
Criteria—40-60 seconds from predicted terrain conflict
Conflict criteria
Within about ¹/₈ mile either side aircraft
The initial distance of ¹/₈ mile (¹/₄ mile wide) expands ±3 from both sides of aircraft as the path is projected forward
Warning Alert
Criteria—20-30 seconds from predicted terrain conflict
Approach & departure
Criteria modified to avoid nuisance alerts

Weather Radar

General

Primarily turbulence avoidance tool
Echoes are from rainfall and water in atmosphere; turbulence is implied
Turbulence mode
Turbulence directly detected by measuring rainfall velocity
Applies to storms within selected range of 40NM or less
Windshear detection
Events detected within 3 NM in front of aircraft
Referred to as predictive windshear
Radar antenna is stabilized with horizon by ADIRU inputs

Weather Radar System

Weather returns displayed in all modes except:
Plan
VOR Centered
Approach Centered
ON/OFF Switch is EFIS WXR map switch
Variable gain settings available in **WX, WX+T** or **MAP** modes
Testing
Weather radar and predictive windshear system may be tested simultaneously
Select **WXR** on EFIS panel and then press **TEST** switch
Activates test of both systems
Scan Pattern
Normal modes— ±90°
Predictive windshear mode below 2300'AGL— ±60°
Tilt—adjustable ±15° from horizon
May be selected differently on L and R sides
If tilt angles are different, an audible "bump" may be heard as antenna angle adjusts
Antenna scan is stabilized only to 40°, so if pitch plus roll exceeds this amount, ground return on one side of the display
Display update
Every sweep if displayed on only one ND
Alternate sweeps if displayed on both NDs
PAC Alert
Annunciation identifies areas of severe attenuation
Indicates signal is attenuated below min discernible signal level
Yellow arc paints on outer edge
Requirements:
Gain control in calibrated position (12 0'clock)
Attenuating position is 80NM or less from A/C
Areas between painted return and PAC alert bar must be avoided
Ground Clutter Suppression (GCS)
Removes approximately 85% of ground clutter targets
Also removes some stationary valid weather returns
Recommended use is temporary for identification of ground targets
Works best with shallow tilt angles of 0-5° tilt down

GPWS Predictive Windshear System (PWS)

System Activation
Enabled during takeoff, approach and landing
Provides immediate alert for the following:
Excessive downdraft or tailwind
Excessive windshear detected ahead of airplane
Master WARNING light accompanies warning
Pressing a master **WARNING** light extinguishes both lights
Windshear alerting is *not* inhibited by pressing master **WARNING**

System Operation

Uses weather radar to detect disturbed air in front of airplane

Weather radar <u>automatically</u> scans in PWS mode when:
> <u>On ground</u> with thrust levers in takeoff range **OR**
> <u>In-flight</u> below 2300' radio altitude

Alerts enabled approximately 12 seconds after scan begins

Prior to takeoff—Alerts can be enabled by pressing WXR switch on EFIS panel

During approach—Alerts enabled below 1200' radio altitude

Radar sweep reduced to ±25° when PWS active

Radar returns only display (even though PWS is active) if WXR switch is selected

PWS Alert Area

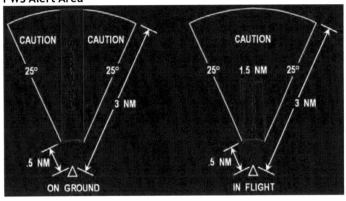

Alert Inhibits

Inhibit Philosophy—Inhibited when:

Operationally unnecessary or inappropriate
> Many alerts indicate abnormal situations only if system is on
> Example—No warning for low oil pressure before engine start

Condition normal for system operation
> Time delays for in transit indications
> Example is valves in transit—no warning to indicate not in commanded position until after time delay

Prevents distraction during takeoff and landing

Voice Annunciation Inhibits

Warnings inhibit related cautions

Voice alerts are prioritized and most important priority messages override lower priorities

Takeoff and Landing Inhibits

Takeoff
> All but most important alerts dealing with engine failure and PWS inhibited from T/O thrust set to V_1
> Inhibits are removed at 400' through 1100' in stages
> <u>Note</u>: *Chart removed from latest OMV2 edition*

Landing
> Inhibits progressively increase below 1500'RA on approach
> Inhibits are removed at 100, 80 and 75 knots

Acronyms

AIMS	airplane information management system
EICAS	engine indication and crew alerting system
GCS	ground clutter suppression
GPWS	ground proximity warning system
PWS	predictive windshear system
TCAS	traffic alert and collision avoidance system

Operational Notes and Lists

Disclaimer: *On this next two pages are lists and consolidated information which have operational relevance.*
These lists are intended as a starting point for consolidating each pilot's personal notes. The reproducible pages following are

For Training Purposes Only

This material is provided in an effort to help in consolidating policy guidelines for planning purposes.
It is <u>not</u> an attempt to replace Operating Manual guidance from which these notes are derived.

Cabin Interphone Notes

Some of the following notes are from an unofficial handout, but the data has been confirmed to work

Normal Calls
- Single hi-lo chime
  EICAS msg: • CABIN CALL

Priority Calls—
- Single hi-lo chime
  EICAS msg: • CABIN ALERT
- Will disconnect a normal priority call

Conference Calls
Normal Conference Call
Calling an individual door (i.e. 71,82, etc.)
Without hanging up, dial another individual door or set of doors

Priority Conference Call
Any cabin station calls
Subsequent station calls of ✱✱ will add that call to the existing priority conference call

Multiple Calls, or clearing Calls when out of sync with incoming calls:
To delete multiple calls in queue use Center CDU
Press DELETE, then line select 1R or line showing the call to be deleted

Cockpit CDU Operations
Call Queue—indicates which station is calling in, i.e.
◆ 71–DOOR 1L ◆ 84–DOOR 4R
etc.

Subsequent calls with indicated door can be added to create a conference call by Line select any handset listed in the call queue to redial selected station and add to call in progress

To dial using CDU
◆ Lift handset
◆ Type door desired
◆ Line select 6L on the CDU

Interphone Directory

	Individual Door Call—All Handsets	
Door 1L & 1R	11	Door 3L & 3R	33

Door 1L & 1R	11	Door 3L & 3R	33
Door 2L & 2R	22	55 / 91	44
Door 1L Only	71	Door 1R Only	81
Door 2L Only	72	Door 2R Only	82
Door 3L Only	73	Door 3R Only	83
Door 4L Only	74	Door 4R Only	84

PA Calls			
PA, 1st Class Only	61	PA, Coach Only	63
PA, Bus. Only	62	PA, All	65
PA, Priority	6✱		

Cabin Only Calls			
Flight Deck	31	Pilot Alert	✱✱
1-Chime Flight Attendant Conference Call			54

Flight Deck Only Calls			
4-Chime Conference Call	/		55 / 91
Pilot Alert Priority CABIN ALERT EICAS Message			✱✱

*** UNOFFICIAL GUIDE—FOR STUDY & PLANNING PURPOSES ONLY

North Atlantic Westbound Route Procedures

- Preflight—
  - Check FMC altitudes on TO page 2
  - Check altimeters +75' of actual, and L to R (RVSM requirement)
  - Fuel freezing temperature—
- Response:ADS CONNECTION Update enroute alternate weather; YQX area WX
- Update winds in FMC: New winds at: 0400, 1000, 1600, 2200Z
- Optional Route 2 Checkpoints (as desired)
- Datalink clearance—Request 60-90 minutes before route entry:G/<Entry Point>/<Time>/<Mach>/<Altitude>
- Example: G/DOTTY/0959/84/35
  FMC PERF page
  - Plot ETPs (i.e. 5450N/-XXX)
  - Plot midpoints:W045-10
  - FMC Alternate page—enter airport 4-character codes
  - Fix page—Enter Alternate with /511 circle for awareness
- If Desired, Enter on message second line: ABLE FLXXX
- Clearance received
- Print / Accept
- Check clearance for accuracy & agreement with filed route
- To review on screen— review [Select message received]
- VNAV Cruise page—set mach to .840 or cleared speed
- Set TCAS to ABOVE on one side, BELOW on the other
  - Altimeter check when level at crossing altitude
  - Position report on coast out frequency
  - Call for HF frequencies & SELCAL on track entry;
  - Tune L and R HFs to check
  - Call and monitor only on one
- Voice: If req'd, call Oceanic Clearance on track msg freq
- *"American <XX> has received datalink oceanic clearance"*
- When Clearance answers:
  "Message sequence number <XXXXX>, estimating <Route Entry Point> at <XXXX>Z"
- On HF:
  American XX, ADS, request SELCAL check <A/C SELCAL Code>"
  "American XX, ADS, Request frequencies, Shanwick next"
  "Gander Radio, American XX, CPDLC, Track X, Request SELCAL check <XX-XX>"
- Circles flight plan oceanic points Verify FMC waypoint names agree with ATC clearance
- CPDLC Logon, 15-45 minutes from oceanic entry point
  - Wait until next point is an oceanic reporting point
  - Select page—DSP <COMM>
  - <ATC> Select
  - LOGON STATUS[] Select
  - LOGON TO: CZQX
  - Check FLIGHT#, TAIL#, AAL#
  - <999> in TIMEOUT not req'd
  - Verify connection:<ATC>
  - Verify ESTABLISHED-XXXX Z
- VHF Frequencies—
  - Set to 121.500 L / 123.450 R
  - 30W—Call Shanwick
  "American XX, CPDLC, Track X, Request SELCAL check <XX-XX>"
  Additional information
  SATCOM—
  Oceanic:Gander 431603   New York 431613
  423201   Shanwick
  Radio: Gndr Dom 431602   Shanwick
  425002
  Santa Maria 426302 New York 436623
  Hibernia oil rig off St. Johns:
  46N 51W   130.27

Takeoff Briefing

The takeoff briefing will be conducted by the Captain (or at the Captain's discretion, the pilot flying) at the gate to include, as a minimum:
- Designate the pilot flying
- Rejected takeoff considerations
- Contingencies, if appropriate:
- Departure procedure (required if not covered previously, or revised by ATC);
- Airport specific engine failure procedure
- Terrain considerations
- Any other taxi / takeoff variables
- Takeoff Alternate
  - Required if weather below lowest active approach minimums that can be flown to an engine out landing
  - 777—Must be within 370 NM of departure airport

Standard Thrust Not Authorized

The following items require Maximum Takeoff Thrust at the TO rating:

Airport Conditions / Weather
- When using Improved Performance
- Windshear is reported or expected.
- When FM_II Airport Advisory requires Maximum Thrust
- Contamination—When runway contaminated by standing water, slush, snow, or ice

The following items require Maximum Takeoff Thrust, but may be used with any thrust rating (TO2, TO1, or TO):
- Weight—If Takeoff Weight (TOW) exceeds Assumed Takeoff Weight (ATOW), New TPS may be obtained authorizing current TOW.
- Weight—If Takeoff Weight (TOW) exceeds Assumed Takeoff Weight (ATOW), New TPS may be obtained authorizing current TOW. TPS 10.3

Autobrakes Required

Must be armed (If operative) for any of the following:
- Runway length 7000 feet or less
- RVR < 4000 or visibility < ¾ mile
  - Setting 2 minimum
  - Setting 3 minimum
- Runway contaminated—standing water/ snow/slush/ice
  - Approach speed is increased above normal by procedure
  - Braking conditions reported less than good
- CAT II and III landings
  - Setting 3 minimum, if operable
- When minimum stopping distance is required—Setting MAX

Note MAX Auto Brake deceleration is slightly less than full manual braking
Recommended: landing with gusty winds or crosswinds

Recommended settings
MAX AUTO—When minimum-stopping distance is required
Deceleration rate is slightly less than that produced by full manual braking
3 or 4—For wet / slippery runways or when landing rollout distance is limited
1 or 2—For moderate deceleration
OM Volume 1, APPROACH–LANDING–GO-AROUND 15.2, 25.11

Auto Speedbrake System

- Will be armed for all landings (If operative)
- Do not land with the Speedbrakes deployed
- Use on Approach
- Use with flaps over 5 causes buffet
- Should be retracted by 1,000 AGL
  OM Volume 1, CLIMB-CRUISE-DESCENT 20.4
- Landing with thrust higher than idle may disable automatic deployment, causing a bounced landing
- If speedbrakes deploy and airplane becomes airborne again,
- They will retract while airborne
- Must then be manually redeployed
  OM Volume 1, APP-LDG-G/A 45.13
- If speedbrakes NOT raised after touchdown, braking effectiveness reduces by up to 60%
  OM Volume 1, APP-LDG-G/A 45.18

Landing Flap Selection

Use of flaps 25 is normally preferred:
- More fuel efficient
- Better noise abatement
- Reduced flap wear
- Improved maneuverability in high (gusty) winds

Note: The 777 not certified for flaps 25 autoland.

Use of flaps 30 is recommended when:
- Tailwind
- Short runway (less than 8000 feet)
- Wet / contaminated runway
- When deemed prudent by the Captain
  OM Volume 1, APP-LDG-G/A15.1

North Atlantic Eastbound Route Procedures

◆ Preflight—
- ♦♦ Check **FMC** altitudes on TO page 2 **600/1000/1000**
- ♦♦ Check altimeters +75' of actual, and L to R (RVSM requirement)
- ♦♦ Fuel freezing temperature—FMC **PERF** page

◆ Datalink clearance—Request 60-90 minutes before route entry **G/<Entry Point>/<Time>/<Mach>/<Altitude>**

◆ Example: **G/DOTTY/0959/84/35**

◆ If Desired, Enter on message second line: **ABLE FLXXX**

◆ Clearance received
- ♦♦ Print / Accept
- ♦♦ Check clearance for accuracy & agreement with filed route
- ♦♦ To review on screen— review▯▯ received▯▯Select message
- ♦♦ Voice: If req'd, call Oceanic Clearance on track msg freq
   "American <XX> has received datalink oceanic clearance"
- ♦♦ When Clearance answers:
   "Message sequence number <XXXXX>, estimating <Route Entry Point> at <XXXX>Z"

◆ Circles flight plan oceanic points Verify FMC waypoint names agree with ATC clearance

◆ CPDLC Logon, 15-45 minutes from oceanic entry point
- ♦♦ Wait until next point is an oceanic reporting point
- ♦♦ Select page—DS? **<COMM>** **<ATC>** Select
- ♦♦ LOGON To: **CZQX**
- ♦♦ Check **FLIGHT#, TAIL#, AAL#**
- ♦♦ **<999>** in **TIMEOUT** not req'd
- ♦♦ Verify connection **<ATC>**
- ♦♦♦ **LOGON STATUS**▯ Select
- ♦♦♦ Verify **ESTABLISHED-XXXX Z**

◆ Response: **ADS CONNECTION**
Update enroute alternate weather; YQX area WX

◆ Update winds in FMC: New winds at: 0400, 1000, 1600, 2200Z
- ♦♦ Plot ETPs (i.e. **5450N/-XXX**)
- ♦♦ Plot midpoints: **W045-10**
- ♦♦ FMC Alternate page—enter airport 4-character codes
- ♦♦ Fix page—Enter Alternate with **/511** circle for awareness

◆ VNAV Cruise page—set mach to .840 or cleared speed

◆ Set TCAS to **ABOVE** on one side, **BELOW** on the other

◆ Altimeter check when level at crossing altitude

◆ Position report on coast cut frequency

◆ Call for HF frequencies & SELCAL on track entry;
- ♦♦ Tune L and R HFs to check
- ♦♦ Call and monitor on one
   "American XX, ADS, Request frequencies, Shanwick next"
- ♦♦ On HF: *"Gander Radio, American XX, ADS, request SELCAL check <A/C SELCAL Code>"*

◆ Set transponder to **2000** 30 minutes after route entry; reminder time in fix page (i.e. **0253Z**)
- ♦♦ VHF Frequencies— Set to 121.500 L / 123.450 R

◆ 30W—Call Shanwick
   "American XX, CPDLC, Track X, Request SELCAL check <XX-XX>"

Additional information

SATCOM—
Oceanic: Gander 431603   New York 431613   Shanwick 423201
Radio: Gndr Dom 431602   Shanwick 425002
Santa Maria 426302 New York 436623

Hibernia oil rig off St. John's: 130.27   46N 51W

Diversion from the NAT or PACOTS System

Setup Notes:

◆ Keep FMC alternate page updated with current enroute alternates.

◆ Have frequencies preset to
- ♦♦ Guard
- ♦♦ Air-Air
- ♦♦ SATCOM 1-Dispatch
- ♦♦ 3SATCOM 2-ATC

◆ PF items are Flying / Navigation items

◆ PNF Items are Administrative / Coordination / Checklist items

◆ Accomplish tasks simultaneously, but keep abreast of actions of other crewmember(s)

Pilot Flying

1) IMMEDIATELY, heading select 60—180 degrees from track heading in the direction towards alternate.
2) Set FL 250 as an initial descent altitude in the MCP altitude.
3) Select FMC VNAV cruise page. Select **ENGOUT**
4) Execute FMC mod
5) Thrust becomes **CON** on good engine Airplane slows to EO speed and begins shallow descent.
6) Select "**ROUTE**" on FMC. Type in 15 mile offset (R15 or L15); Execute
7) Call for appropriate Checklist.
8) If not below floor of track system by offset, turn to parallel track in direction towards alternate.
9) When offset achieved, modify VNAV EO cruise page.
   a) Select Company Speed, which enters .84 / 320 knots
   b) This will increase descent rate and get you below tracks sooner
   c) Consider FLCH until below tracks, then back to VNAV
      Note: Time and fuel to alt are now accurate after speed change.
   d) Note max EO altitude and reset MCP altitude; Execute
10) Level off between FL's, i.e., FL235, 225, etc. and below MAX CO Speed altitude sustainable
11) When below tracks, select ALT page and select divert now to your alternate and Execute. This will:
   a) Turn you on direct course to ALT (**LNAV** press).
   b) Make Stars and Approaches at alt airport available on **DEPT/ARR** page.

Pilot Not Flying

1) Turn on all exterior aircraft lights
2) Call "Mayday" on 121.5 and 123.45
3) Call "Mayday" on ATC {HF, VHF, or SATCOM) and get clearance to alternate
4) Seatbelt signs-ON
5) Transponder to 7700
6) Call additional crewmember to cockpit if not yet accomplished
7) Brief F / A ´s--Advise dispatch-Get WX
8) You'll have ●COMM; Touch COMM— Diversion Message is displayed

Titles Currently Available
By Rick Townsend

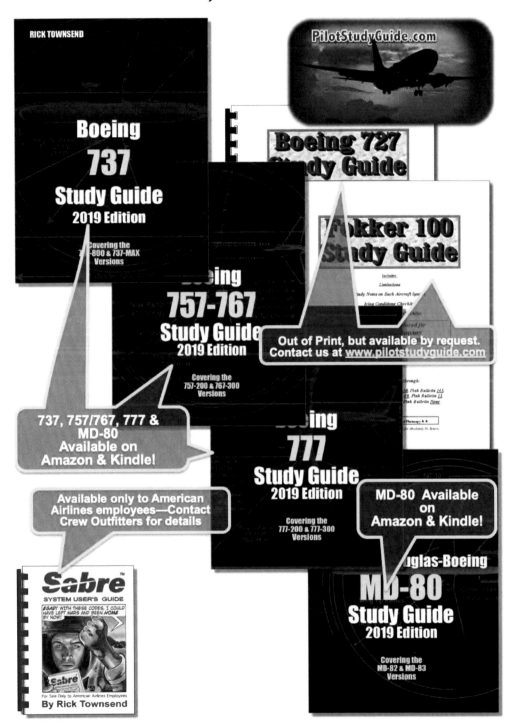

To purchase any of these titles, go to Crew Outfitters locations at the Flight
Academy Gift Shop, or at DFW Airport Terminal C Operations
To purchase online, go to *www.crewoutfitters.com*

To order by phone, call **800-874-1204**

This book is available through Amazon in both Kindle and in print format!

Giving Back

A portion of the proceeds from every book help support some worthy charities. Here are two of the charities your book purchase supports:

Kenya Kids Can!
Feeding and teaching world changers of tomorrow

Kenya Kids Can is a non-profit working in the Rift Valley of Kenya. They feed students and construct solar powered computer centers to improve education and bring hope to needy students. Please browse the website to learn about what can be done to truly change lives.

www.kenyakidscan.org

Snowball Express

Serving the *children* of our fallen military heroes

Snowball Express Could Use Your Help!

Snowball Express honors America's fallen military service members who have made the ultimate sacrifice since 9/11 by

♦ **Humbly serving the families they left behind**

♦ **Championing their children's future success by creating opportunities for joy, friendship, and communal healing**

♦ **Connecting these families to one another.**

Since 2006, the mission of Snowball Express has been a simple, yet profoundly important one: Providing hope and new happy memories to the children of military fallen heroes who have died while on active duty since 9/11. In December each year we bring children together from all over the world for a four-day experience filled with fun activities, like sporting events, dances, amusement parks and more.

Nationally, Snowball Express provides comprehensive support programs for fallen families that are focused on transition and connections to community resources, healing and wellness, peer engagement, education and personal/professional development programs.

www.snowballexpress.org